The Way of
Knockdown

Gary Chamberlain

ISBN: 1490334785
ISBN-13: 978-1490334783

Text copyright © 2013 Gary Chamberlain
Cover illustration by kind permission of Rod Ter Weijden
Thanks to Karen van Wyk for assisting with formatting this book.

To my family for their love and support

And with thanks to all my instructors.

Table of Contents

Introduction

Do (way) in Japanese implies a spiritual path. The ways offer something internal, rather than the wealth, trophies or popular recognition sought by champions in western sports. My *way* was through knockdown.

I have not attempted to present an A to Z guide to winning tournaments. There are many fine training books available by famous fighters. Many of my memories show acute human failings and my route had many detours and dead-ends along the way. I hope these all contribute to the overall story. All lives have struggles and rising above them is what it's all about.

In an effort to record things accurately I have cross checked these pages with other people who were training at the time, although there are now few of us left still practising regularly. Any inaccuracies are my responsibility, but I hope you will excuse them as many of these events occurred long ago. Memories of specific details fade over time, although the lessons remain.

Note: The use of karate titles can be confusing and repetitious, particularly for non Martial Artists. I have therefore kept them to a minimum. No disrespect is intended.

Osu! (A word used strongly in and out of the dojo to convey respect)

Foreword

Kyokushin has always had a fierce reputation for being a tough system of karate where no quarter is asked and none given and I think that's why I admire it so much. The training is strong, uncomplicated and deliciously honest. It's also savagely effective, let us be in no doubt of that. In an age where the populists and the unqualified like to lambast traditional martial arts as being antiquated and ineffective I think it is wise to remember that some of the toughest martial artists walking this spinning planet, some of the people I admire most, find their roots in Japanese karate.

And Gary Chamberlain is one of them. I admire him very much, because he too is direct, uncomplicated and strong. And he is very effective. That is why I heartily recommend him and endorse this inspiring book about Gary's personal odyssey through a bullied and skinny childhood to a senior, rock solid martial artist of the first order.

Geoff Thompson Coventry, England 2009

Skinny and Scared

I was born in a small cottage in Warwickshire in 1956. My father had recently left the Royal Marines, where he had been an instructor at their Devon training base. During his service he had represented them in modern pentathlon, so with his equine knowledge he found employment on leaving as a groom in a hunting stable. By the time I was two years old we had moved to Tur Langton, a small village in South Leicestershire.

Home life was really happy for the first few years. This was a safer age when children were allowed to roam free, with everyone in the village looking out for them. At the time the village had half a dozen working farms with a variety of workers cottages, two pubs, a church, a red phone box and a village hall. My father worked for the Johnson's but I was allowed free access everywhere and spent hours outdoors playing with the other children. I liked nothing more than helping my father with the horses. If he was in a good mood, I sometimes got to ride the huge heavy hunters on a lead rein as they were taken out for their morning exercise. As a youngster, it was the most fantastic feeling in the world. Cold and frosty early morning rides in the rolling English countryside are hard to beat.

Unfortunately, my father's violence was the downside. Life was pretty strict - almost military - in many ways. He ruled the house with an iron fist and everything had to be shipshape. My mother, a kind and gentle woman, took the brunt of things if he lost his temper. Once it went, he would rain blows on me with whatever came to hand if I stayed within reach. This happened rarely, but I quickly learnt the feeling of fear. I don't want to overstate this and I know a lot of kids had things far worse than me, but I soon worked out that when faced with violence the best option was to run away from it and hide. This was to rebound on me at a later stage of my childhood.

On starting at Church Langton Primary School I was already a tough little kid and held my own easily in the playground. The head teacher, Captain Hill, was a sadist who liked nothing better than thrashing kids with his 'bottom knocker', a plastic tennis racket that stung like hell but cleverly left no bruises. I got it on the first day for scrapping and laughed at him. Compared to my father's blows it was a mere tickle. This incensed him and for years after I was thrashed for things other kids seemed to get away with. I'd never cry though so I think I denied him his greatest pleasure.

I spent hours on my bike and rode for miles every day. The roads were far safer then so I travelled all over the place with friends from school. Cycling got me away from the house, which was an added bonus, and I enjoyed the exercise. As I moved on to Kibworth High School I rode there every day and on going up to Market Harborough Grammar School I cycled if the weather was good. It was perhaps natural that by the time I was fourteen I had started to race bikes, doing regular time trials with the Welland Valley Wheelers. I had a '10 speed racer' but for some reason I loved fixie's and trained regularly at the Saffron Lane cycle track in Leicester. Fixed wheel bikes are great for fitness and I could soon ride hard and fast for hours. But for an unfortunate misunderstanding I'd have kept this going and never even started training in karate.

By then I had an enterprising little business going washing the village cars and combined with paper rounds and odd jobs I was earning my own cash. I wanted a really good track bike and rang up about one advertised in the local paper. I went over to see it and put down a deposit. One of the other group members had seen the same advert, decided he wanted it, and demanded I withdrew my interest to let him buy it for himself. He was from a wealthy family and was spoilt rotten, so my refusal really annoyed him. This caused a split in the group and I soon found myself out in the cold. I could have coped with that but things rapidly took a turn for the worse.

This was at the start of the 'skinhead' era in the UK, with gangs of bored kids hanging around and 'putting the boot in' to anyone who crossed them. With long floppy hair I was different from the crowd. While in the school 'cycling' gang this was never a problem, but on becoming a bit isolated trouble soon came to visit. It started small, the odd shove here and there, but I found very quickly that the threat of violence brought the same fear response my father had ingrained in me. Self-preservation was all I knew. This was no longer playground scuffles, some kids took serious beatings. The school took little interest in bullying, preferring to think that the odd bloody nose would make men of us. I wasn't at all convinced that being nutted then kicked to bits would build character, so while I would fight if cornered I avoided it like the plague. I became withdrawn and even joined the chess club to avoid the risk of violence at lunchtime. (I reached a good standard and like to think it has helped in later life.) Despite that, my general confidence sank really low. Word spread, and soon even the thugs from lower years with shaved heads and Dr Marten boots were trying it on to make a name for themselves. Something had to be done.

My mother urged me to keep out of trouble while my father's response was to show me brutal military unarmed combat. The moves he showed me were very effective and I've never forgotten them, but they were completely inappropriate for the school playground. In my case the problem wasn't just physical it was mainly psychological, so my mother eventually recognised something longer term was required. My great uncle was a Judo black belt so she enlisted his help. I was taken to the local Judo *dojo* (training hall) but cycling had kept me rapier thin and at 6 feet tall I weighed just over eight stone. It obviously wasn't for me. The coach was about 5 feet tall and built like a dump truck. He looked at my skinny build and politely suggested I think again.

Next she tried the local boxing club, but sparring there was arranged by height so I faced being punched about by adults. Most of the kids training there had broken noses and looked well the worse for wear. I noticed some of the school skinheads there, eyeing me up with huge sneers on their gap toothed faces. No fun in that, in fact if that was my choice I'd have happily run the gauntlet every day at school rather than *knowing* I'd get a beating twice a week at the gym.

She then enquired about karate. I'd heard of this but like most other people thought it was about breaking bricks with weird shrieks and grunts, but as by now things were getting serious at school I was game to try anything. We went up to watch the Leicester Karate Kyokushinkai training on a bitterly cold November night. Despite this, everyone was pouring with sweat. I liked the respectful atmosphere and looking at the kicks I realised I had a natural head-start. I had very long legs, so I could visualise myself kicking high very easily. I imagined my tormentors felled by my devastating high kicks and signed up in November 1971, little realising the whole direction of my life would now change.

Early Training

My father just scoffed. He had been to the Far East while in the Royal Marines and spent time in Japan during the Korean War. He told tales of bar-room brawls on the waterfront where by his account the UN 'peacekeepers' quickly overcame any local opposition. He disliked Orientals in general after witnessing very unpleasant things in Korea and that twisted his thinking. He simply couldn't understand why any Englishman would want to learn 'sport' from them. To him, unarmed combat delivered with extreme aggression was far more effective. For life and death struggles, I agree. But for now I wanted something effective but controlled. Something to build back my self-belief.

While his blinkered attitude didn't put me off, it did make life difficult straight away. My mother couldn't get him to help, so she paid for my membership fees and *gi* (suit) from her meagre

Christmas savings. In return for this she made me promise to stick at it for a year. I would pay my own fees, have to cycle to and from the club and would be allowed no excuses. I was brought up to seal a bargain with a firm handshake and eye contact and if I made a promise there was no going back. My father snorted at this saying, 'He's far too bloody weak to stick at anything'. That was the greatest thing he ever (unwittingly) did for me. Not only was I up against it now at school, but pride was at stake at home as well. I made the pledge to my mother and gritted my teeth, now absolutely determined to prove him wrong.

Training was on Tuesday and Thursday evenings and the occasional Sunday morning at an old Territorial Army base. I'd cycle the 5 miles home from school, grab some tea and immediately set off for the dojo 15 miles away. The route there was hilly so it was pretty rough. It was a harsh winter and usually cold, windy and pouring with rain. On arrival I had to change into my new gi and trainers to run round the drill yard 20 times - another 5 miles. We then shivered together in the changing room until class started. The dojo was in an old garage about thirty feet square. The floor was covered in wooden battens with hardboard nailed on top. These often came loose so the instructor walked around with a hammer before and even during training knocking down any sharp edges that had started to stick out before anyone ripped their feet apart. The roof was corrugated iron over a riveted steel frame, so the first *kiai* (shout) of the night sent a brown mist of rust and other debris showering down on us. Training was from 7:00 until 10:00pm, after which I had to put my cold wet clothes back on and cycle back home again. To say this was tough was an understatement.

People often ask me if mental strength is trainable or if it's something we're born with. To me it hinges on the stubbornness to press on despite problems. I soon knew I had plenty of that as I proved it by doing the whole year, as promised, without missing any sessions. Would I have carried on if I'd not made that promise? I doubt it. It was very tough and all through that first winter I cursed my stupidity for giving my word. Memories of my father scoffing at me spurred me on though, and by the end of that first year I absolutely loved it.

Training was direct, uncomplicated and strong. Basic techniques were repeated hundreds of times each and stance work was done over and over again. *Kata* (formal exercises) were then followed by the dreaded *kumite* (free-fighting). Those still capable afterwards finished off with push-ups, sit-ups and squats. The format rarely varied but if it did it was only for something worse. Particular favourites were half an hour of bunny hops or such like to test our 'spirit.' The training methodology could best be described as deranged. If doing 50 of an exercise was considered good for you, doing 500 was the order of the day. The dropout rate was huge, but those who stayed got surprisingly resilient to hard training. The sparring was positively cruel by today's standards. Rules were pretty much ignored and there was a lot of latitude allowed with contact levels. There was little emphasis on stylish flowing combinations; it was more about stalking the opponent, feinting to make an opening and then putting everything into single techniques. Literally trading blow for blow. We blocked so hard our arms were constantly bruised. We never wore pads, and all targets were allowed. Face punches were supposed to be controlled but often weren't, and groin kicks (although we wore cricket boxes) regularly dropped people to their knees. We were not allowed to step back to avoid contact and blood meant absolutely nothing. One of the instructors, Ted Smith, was as hard as nails and absolutely merciless. He thought nothing of pinning you up against the wall and hammering in savage body punches until you fell to the floor. More 'character building' I suppose, but at least in the dojo the beating stopped if you went to the ground. No mercy was given or received so I soon learnt to keep people at a distance with my kicks. With my skinny frame, letting people body punch me was always very painful and had to be avoided at all costs.

The other instructor, Pete Kisby, was a lot more technical and rather more controlled. He at least took the time to explain things a bit more, while Ted just went to town on you. Ted was even harder on people who caught him back with a good shot, so again that familiar dread emerged. *Should I fight back and risk an even harder beating? Or go easy and hope he lets me off the hook?* I settled on a pragmatic approach. Until my skills improved I went easy and quickly learnt to grab any partner for sparring except Ted. I spent hours working on key skills at home, and invented several novel training methods. One favourite was cutting a large square out of the side of a cardboard box and practising punching in and out at full speed. As I got more accurate I made the hole smaller with tape until it was only just wider than my fist. This helped my punches get sharper and more accurate. For kicking I loved going into a muddy field and cutting the heads from a few cabbages. I then put them up on sticks and practised kicking them off, wearing my father's old hobnail boots for a bit of extra difficulty. This improved my balance and speed until eventually I could explode a cabbage at well over six feet high with a fast roundhouse kick from either foot. I now felt ready to stand my ground and start giving people a bit back. Sadly, by that time Ted Smith and Pete Kisby had fallen out and Ted had left the club for good. I never found out the full details, but Ted, like my father, helped me a lot by giving me that extra motivation.

First Competitions

That first winter took forever but I soon adapted to the demands. I found a good chippie on my way home, where the owner obviously felt sorry for me. I'd turn up as he was closing shop and he'd wrap any unsold stuff in a newspaper for a few pence. I'd wash it all down with a can of coke before heading back. I passed my first belt in the spring and even started to time the cycle rides to and from training. As the weather improved so did the pleasure, while my 'special' diet started to put on a few pounds.

In the summer I passed my orange belt* and started to feel more capable. Regular sparring had sharpened me up and my kicks were already dangerous due to my extra-curricular training. I could never understand people who moaned about being a poor kicker but did nothing outside the dojo. Even at 16 I understood that you have to graft if you want to improve.

We turned up for training one night to be told we were having a competition against a London club the next Sunday. I was surprised to see my name on the list. Questions about rules were just answered with a shrug and, 'You'll be fine.'

Our team captain was Stuart Crewe, who was the coolest and most precise fighter in the dojo. On the day we lined up, bowed, and then sat down with Stuart going up first against a black belt opponent. Stuart was a blue belt but this was in the days when black belts were untouchable so we half expected things to go badly. After a brief exchange the black belt blocked a front kick, grabbed Stuart's gi and elbowed him straight in the face. He was understandably stunned, and while he stood there with his nose pouring blood, the black belt gave him another one for good measure, knocking him down. He was picked up, tissue was rammed up his nose and the referee announced, *'Wazari!'* (Half point) A few moments later, 'Time!' was called.

What the hell am I doing here? Crossed my mind, but by now the second fight had started. We were already one fight down, but two minutes later the scores were level. I was up next, and lost in record time as I tried two front kicks which my opponent easily blocked and countered to score with reverse punches. I sat down shaking violently. I knew nothing then about adrenaline and such like so I just thought it was because I was scared stiff. A win would have boosted my confidence, but of course losing raised serious doubts. The team lost, but everyone - even Stuart - agreed it had been worthwhile. Another was soon arranged with a northern dojo for a few weeks time. This time we did better, winning by three fights to two. My opponent was a green belt and I managed to score twice in quick succession by flicking up a fast high roundhouse kick with the front leg and nailing him with a back kick as he tried to counter. I had managed to win and it felt great!

The next one was the big one. The British Championships were to be held at the Barking Assembly Halls. I wasn't picked but travelled with the team to offer support. We went there confident enough, but were blown away 5:0 by the Dagenham Club of Ticky Donovan. (He later left Kyokushin to found Ishinryu and eventually become the British All-Styles Coach.) It was obvious to me that although we fought hard at Leicester, at that time we simply weren't doing the right things for this type of competition. My first thought was to visit clubs that fought 'points' style and get some tips but choice locally was a bit limited. The Shotokan did mainly kata and the Shukokai just seemed to flick their techniques about, quite the opposite to us - we were expected to be working full-on all the time. I travelled to some other Kyokushin clubs, but they were just like us, heavy training and heavy contact. I wanted to win so decided to investigate other ways of training.

The British Karate Kyokushinkai (BKK) originally used the Judo belt system of white, yellow, orange, green, blue and brown belt. This later changed in line with Japan to white, blue, yellow, green and brown, with two kyu (levels) at each belt, in 1973

Japanese 'Instruction'

One of the earliest karate magazines available in the UK was *Karate and Oriental Arts.* I was reading it one day at school in a boring history lesson, and saw an article about a Japanese instructor in London named Meiji Suzuki, who taught a different style - Wado Ryu. On asking about it at the dojo most said it was crap, but one remarked it was very good for competition fighting. That lit a bulb in my head so with the naivety of youth I decided to go there and see what it was like. I had a school holiday coming up where keeping out of my father's way was always a consideration, so I decided to go to London (100 miles away). I hitched a lift, a common enough thing for young people to do at the time. This was a simpler age, long before mobile phones and being able to update parents on your whereabouts. At 14 my father had given me a front door key and said, 'Don't wake me up if you come in late.' They were used to me stopping out at friends houses so I didn't bother telling them my plans.

I set off early and arrived in the centre of London after just a couple of lifts. A lorry driver dropped me off near St. Pancras station, just a short walk from the dojo on the corner of Judd Street and Cromer Street. By now I had been promoted to green belt, and so walked in bold as brass asking when the senior class was to be held. Suzuki eyed me up suspiciously and asked my grade. On telling him, he then lectured me about modesty for ten minutes and told me to report to the beginner class 45 minutes later. I had nowhere to go so hung around and stretched in the changing rooms. A few students came in and seemed cheerful enough, and at the appointed time we filed upstairs to the dojo.

The class passed through without drama, although it was a lot slower than I was used to. We were then told to partner up for sparring. Anxious to show that I should have been given the benefit of the doubt, I tore into my opponent and dropped him with a front kick without further ceremony. Suzuki was furious. There was a trainee instructor there from Greece, who was told to partner me next. I swept him easily, which again didn't please Suzuki. To my amazement he then stepped up himself. I still didn't think I'd done anything wrong. Fighting in Leicester was always very rough, and as I'd not damaged anyone permanently, just embarrassed them, I thought nothing of it.

Suzuki, a 5th Dan 'All-Japan Universities Champion' (or whatever he was) then proceeded to beat the crap out of me. After about ten minutes he'd vented his anger and I was in a pretty poor state. My legs and ribs were badly bruised, my teeth were loose and my lips were split from his face punches. He just bowed with a sick smile, checked himself in the mirror and walked out of the dojo. I was now in serious trouble as I could hardly walk. I had hoped to get the tube as far as the bottom of the M1 and then hitch lifts until I got home, but this was now impossible. Luckily one of his students saw it all and kindly let me stop over at his place. His girlfriend cooked us a meal and as I was still limping the next day, he put me on the train back to Leicester after I promised to post back my train fare.

My father was furious. Not because I'd gone to London without his permission, but because this highly trained adult had beaten me up. For all his faults if anyone else hurt us he'd have fought to the death. It was all my mother could do to stop him going to London and putting Suzuki in hospital. I for one would've paid good money to see him put his 'unarmed combat vs. mere sport' theory to the test. He eventually calmed down, but it just proved (to him) that his low opinion of karate - and Orientals - was right on the money. I must admit I began to wonder if he was right. It would be many years later before I saw a truly positive side to Japanese style instruction.

(I saw Suzuki some fifteen years later at the BKK Tournament. He was right out of shape, but still just as arrogant. I reminded him who I was and offered him a return match in the car park. He went as white as a sheet and hurried off. Not the best example of the way of the warrior)

Problem Solved

I returned to school after the holidays having passed my 'O' levels and moved up to the sixth form. I had a sharp mind and found most subjects easy so my teachers anticipated good results. I hoped to take 'A' levels and then go on to University. I then hoped to get a short career commission in the Royal Navy (not realising kids from poor families rarely did) so Maths, Physics and English were my chosen subjects.

I was walking up to school one day and saw someone near the gates on a brand new motorbike. As I got closer I realised it was one of my former tormentors who had left at the end of the previous year. He had got a job in a factory and come back to show off his new toy, standing there surrounded by an admiring gang. As I drew level he made a snide remark, which got his mates giggling. I expected my stomach to start churning as adrenaline again began running riot, but the strangest thing happened.

I was laser focussed and deadly calm. Memories of Suzuki flashed through my mind as I read the name on his motorcycle tank and I thought *I've sparred with a Japanese champion. I can handle this twat.*

I turned back towards him and said, 'What did you say?' He looked smug but didn't answer. I took a step closer and asked, 'What did you *fucking* say?' with twice the malice.

He now looked concerned and went to get off his motorbike. I waited until he was half off and threw a vicious front kick. Maybe it was nerves, maybe it was temper, but it missed his stomach and caught him full in the face. He sprawled over backwards taking his precious motorcycle over with him. People told me later I still had my briefcase in one hand and my lunch in the other. I turned and walked away. His 'friends' shrank back to let me pass. I felt twelve feet tall!

Word spread quickly. I noticed groups in the assembly hall looking and pointing, and instantly thought, *Oh God, I'm in for it now. Everybody will want to have a go.* But to my surprise, nothing happened. From that day to leaving school nine months later I never had a whisper of trouble. A teacher even had a quiet word with me, and while not condoning brawling in any way, he congratulated me on standing up for myself and asked what I had been learning.

When I said, 'karate sir,' he went deathly pale and ushered me straight out of his office. I found out years later he had been in Burma in the Second World War and wouldn't even buy a Japanese TV, so badly had he been treated.

A few weeks later the school had its annual cross-country challenge. The year before I had come 158th, but with the benefit of a year's hard training I came 5th. I had also started to fill out and gained about 28lbs. I never talked about karate at school so had not been asked to explain or demonstrate anything to friends. That kept things mystical and served me well. As far as I knew no one else in the whole school was training, or maybe they did what I did and kept it under their hat. It was a whole fresh start, and things were finally looking up.

Leaving Home

The next year flew past. I trained harder than ever at the dojo and now looked forward to the 'holidays'. I had found work in a timber mill for the summer and was looking forward to putting money in the bank. Until then I'd scratched around washing cars and the like for pin money, but the promise of a man's wages was something to look forward to. By the end of the holidays I was dog tired. Lifting huge off-cuts of timber all day and stacking them high was building my strength, but the long hours and overtime had left me drained. I came back late one night to find my parents arguing. Things got heated, and I could see the warning signs. Instead of beating a hasty retreat for some reason I stayed around, and when my father eventually lost his temper I stood between them.

I was now seventeen and he had roughed me up me for years under the guise of 'toughening me up' but I now decided to make a stand. Tempers were lost, words exchanged and blows struck. Once the dust had settled he just glared at me, but I already knew what was coming. We had crossed the line and I'd have to leave home. I couldn't wait. Crap you put up with as a kid rapidly gets tedious as you get older.

I went upstairs, put a few things in a bag (my karate kit first) and rang my sister to ask if she'd put me up for a few days. It took forty-five minutes on the bus to get to her house, so I reflected bitterly on my change of circumstances. Later that week I went back to pick up some more of my things. My father was adamant that I was at fault for intervening and he now washed his hands of me. Fine by me, I'd had enough of him too. My sister was happy for me to stay for a while, but as she was struggling to run her own house, I'd have to pay my own way. I reluctantly dropped ideas of 'A' levels, University, and the Royal Navy and picked up the local paper to look for a job.

Two phone calls later I was an apprentice toolmaker. It wasn't my ideal career choice but I needed work and they accepted me on the spot. I often wish I'd rang up an accountants or lawyers instead. The apprenticeship was part machine shop and part theory, with the first college part due to start a week later. I would earn the princely sum of £15.53 pence per week. £5.00 for my sister, who would provide cereal and toast for breakfast and an evening meal, and £10.53 for me. Happy with that, I picked up my bag and went training. Luckily, her house was only a fifteen minute walk from the dojo, which had by now moved to the Highfields area of Leicester. We had been stopped from using the Territorial Army centre following action on the mainland by the IRA. I remember thinking; *it's not all bad! At least I won't have to graft all day then cycle up to training!*

Moat Boys School

Moat Boys was an old Victorian school right in the middle of Highfields. This was a formerly prosperous area with grand old Victorian villas, but now rather run down and shabby with a reputation for drugs and prostitution. It was home to large immigrant communities of Muslims on the one hand and West Indians on the other. The Muslims kept themselves to themselves while the West Indians were far more outgoing. Within weeks we had recruited lots of new members and most were naturally very athletic. They really brought a new lease of life to the club and training took on a new intensity. Most were really streetwise and natural fighters. The sparring in the club improved no end and I made some great friends.

As an added bonus I was then always welcomed in pubs and clubs in Leicester that - rightly or wrongly - were seen as 'black' pubs where white guys rarely went unless they wanted a fight. I never felt unsafe in Highfields. Once the street girls and pimps knew you were a local they left you alone. If I saw a gang coming towards me, chances were high that at least one would be training so I never had any trouble. As a seventeen year old from a small village I had a lot of living to do and those days in Highfields, with new friends at college and at the dojo were absolutely great.

Summer Camp

Another year rushed past. I worked, ate, trained and slept with plenty of socialising for good measure. I went down to London in March and passed my brown belt in a tough grading in front of some senior instructors. While waiting to go in one of the other hopefuls, Cyril Andrews, asked if I was going to 'Summer Camp'. 'I don't know,' I replied, 'what's that all about?' He explained that the previous year there had been a European Summer Camp in Holland where two senior Japanese Instructors had led the training. 'Was it good?' I asked innocently. 'Brilliant,' he replied. *Right!* I thought, *sign me up*.

A few months later I took a train to Harwich where I met up with a crowd of fellow karate-ka. We had already got on the ferry when a very different story started to emerge. Apparently the year before the Japanese instructors had been unhappy with the spirit shown by the Europeans, and proceeded to lay into them as they saw fit with their *shinai*. These are split cane swords used in Kendo practise with a leather collar to adjust the tension. They were normally used for 'testing' in certain kata, and when set as hard as iron and in the hands of an expert they left massive bruises on their victims. This gave me a real dilemma. As a child I had been beaten more than enough and on leaving home I had promised myself I would suffer no man to ever hit me like that again. On mentioning this to a fellow brown belt he just grimaced. 'What will you do then?' He asked. 'Tell them to b-back off,' was my slightly nervous reply. 'You can't do that, they're both *Shihans*.' (Senior instructors) 'So what?' I responded, 'Nobody, and I mean nobody, is going to beat me with a stick.' 'We'll see,' he said, sounding very subdued.

I later noticed the BKK chief instructor; *Sensei* (Teacher) Steve Arneil was also looking worried. Word had spread about the beatings and quite a few said, 'No way!' He tried to calm people down by explaining it was just another form of training, the idea being to take the blow without losing your focus.

This sounded plausible enough, but for myself I just knew that if anyone hit me with a stick I'd react very badly. It wasn't about the pain, it was simply the thought of standing there taking it with no right of reply - as I'd done as a child -

which I strongly objected to. I didn't care two hoots if this was 'normal' training in Japan. I would have done my level best to wrestle it from him and shove it in his eye rather than meekly stand there and be beaten, and to hell with the consequences. I counted on someone intervening if it came to that. If not, the worst they could do was knock me down and I'd had plenty of that already at home.

On arrival we were ushered off to our tents on the edge of the field and then back to the main building for food and a briefing. The schedule was outlined, along with the 'do's' and 'don'ts'.

'Always stand when a Shihan comes near you.'

'Always say Osu! Very strongly if they give a command.'

'Always move out of their way if they're walking past.'

'Never look directly at them.'

I found that last one really strange. For as long as I could remember, my father had drilled into me that we should hold our head up, give a firm handshake and smile. I was an Englishman and that was the English way. Suddenly this whole Summer Camp thing seemed a very poor idea. A little later a Limo arrived and out they stepped. One short and very stocky - Tadashi

Nakamura - and one quite tall - Shigeru Oyama. Steve Arneil greeted them very respectfully, and after a brief introduction the rest of the camp, bar the instructors, were dismissed and told to report at 6:00am on the main field for morning training. Few slept well.

In the morning we all lined up nervously in our gi and running shoes and waited, and waited; and waited. Eventually one of the junior instructors took us running and through a hard circuit routine until we broke off for breakfast. *Not too bad,* I thought, *I can handle this.* The Shihans appeared in the breakfast hall looking bleary eyed and grumpy. Apparently they had drunk themselves senseless the night before and were severely hung over. Steve Arneil was visibly nervous and no-one envied his position. As the most senior British instructor everyone would look to him to intervene if the Shihans got too spiteful, but looking at his subservient body language I wasn't sure he was up to the task.

The morning session was followed by basics, with each grade separated into groups and drilled by the nervous instructors. Tadashi Nakamura prowled around like a leopard looking for a lame animal, while Shigeru Oyama repeatedly smacked his shinai into the ground as if practising his cuts ready for the weakest of the bunch. He walked past the black belt group and shouted loud enough for everyone to hear.

'Black belts! You shit!' This seemed to cheer him up a bit so he then wandered over to our brown belt group, pointed back and shouted, 'Black belts! They shit! Brown belts! You shit! Try be better shit than them!'

To say I was disappointed was an understatement. I had hoped to be inspired, but what I saw was just two extremely tough men who appeared to be worse bullies than I'd ever known before. As it was the hope of overcoming bullies that motivated me to start training, I just felt the wheel had simply turned a full circle. Tough guys that chuck their weight around are two a penny and I've never been impressed by that.

The days continued in the same vein but strangely, by the end of the week everyone had pulled together, united by their dislike of the Shihans and we even started to enjoy ourselves. The Shihans eventually showed a slightly more human side, even taking on and beating all comers on the air hockey table to rousing applause. It was only on the very last day that we saw their true potential. On a photo shoot they started to spar. Lightly at first, but gradually building up the pace. Cameras clicked away, but they were so fast that every photograph I took was just a blur. Remarkable. Their ability was fantastic, but we'd seen nothing all week except arrogance and disdain.

How different things could have been if they'd just understood and accepted that Europeans work harder when inspired. Steve Arneil had in fact stepped up to the challenge and persuaded them not to beat anybody, but the implied threat alone still got everyone on edge as soon as they wandered nearby. I took and passed my 1st kyu at the end of the week, and despite my earlier misgivings I found myself already looking forward to the next year, where I now hoped to take my black belt test.

I returned to work after my 'holiday'. I had passed the first year of college and the practical assessments easily enough, but by now I hated it. College was a good laugh, as I had great friends there, but the factory work was dire. I got there at 7:00am and stood at a machine all day. It was highly skilled work with very fine tolerances, but even so I was bored. I also hated the smell of 'suds', the miller's oil used on the lathes and cutting machines. It got everywhere. Your clothes stank, your hair stank, and it got right into your skin and took a scrubbing brush to remove. I badly wanted out but had signed a contract. Luckily for me, the Government was soon to intervene.

In 1974 the miners and power workers tried to hold the Government to ransom with strike action and the country was soon on its knees. Power was lost and production in industry cut to three days a week to conserve energy. My firm helped its craftsmen by keeping them on full wages, but the apprentices instantly had their wages cut to three fifths. On that, I could no longer afford to live, but as they had now technically broken the terms of my employment, I was free to look for work elsewhere.

Fire Brigade

By now I'd got to know Pete Kisby more personally. As he was twelve years my senior it would be stretching things to say we were close friends, but I respected him and soaked up his instruction and general advice like a sponge. I also spent time at his house, located on the estate of Fire Service houses around the Central Fire Station in Leicester. I was without question one of his keenest students, as despite any obstacles that life put in my way I very rarely missed training. As I was now financially desperate I went to see him intending to ask if he'd consider letting me train for free until I got a better job and paid him back. His advice was better than anything I could have hoped for. Why didn't I join the Fire Brigade?

He explained that the City and County Brigades were amalgamating, and at the same time reducing the weekly hours from 56 to 48 hours a week. This meant many more Firemen had to be recruited, who were now being allowed to live away from the estate, once a pre-condition of employment. I had often watched them training and it looked brilliant, but had never seriously considered joining before as I was committed to finishing my apprenticeship. Financial considerations were now changing all that.

I applied, passed an interview and physical test and on 16th December 1974 became Fireman 340 Chamberlain for the next 31 years. This isn't the story of my Fire Service career, but I will return to it at intervals later to illustrate how my attitudes and mental strength changed over time. I completed my basic training - which the discipline of both home and karate had prepared me well for - and started my service on 'D' section. My sister's new boyfriend had by now moved in, so as I had changed career and was earning more money, I got my own flat and started building up seriously for my black belt test.

Black Belt

'You're not ready.' 'But it's been twelve months since I got 1st kyu.' 'I don't care. I decide when you take your black belt, and I say you're not ready.' I had trained really hard since the last summer camp. Since joining the Fire Service I was eating constantly and handling heavy equipment. I never used weights, but despite that I was now eleven and a half stones and very, very fit. I had put on three stone since I started training and was getting quite strong. I had even started shaving! I was off to Holland again in a few weeks and asked Pete if I could take my black belt test. I was puzzled at his response. He offered no explanation. Since I started I had either passed or caught up with every other member, as during that time no-one else from Leicester had tried for their black belt. I was a bit crestfallen, so went off to Holland with the wind well and truly taken out of my sails.

As soon as I got on the boat, everyone started asking if I was going for black belt. When I answered 'No!' it inevitably led to, 'Why not?' until I got bored with telling everyone Pete had refused me permission. After a few days training though, I heard from one of the senior black belts in the British group that Steve Arneil had said I should go for it. I naturally assumed permission from the BKK chief instructor over-ruled Pete's earlier refusal, and happily stuck my name down. The test was all I'd expected and more. We did three hours of basics and kata, followed by very hard fighting with some giant Dutchmen. (We were still fighting 'points' style while the Dutch already fought 'knockdown') To my delight, and the obvious pleasure of the British group, I passed with flying colours.

I had trained really hard for this, and my first thought was that I hoped I'd made my mother proud. Her sacrifices a few years before had now really paid off. Even my father congratulated me. His doctor had by now diagnosed that his mood swings were caused by clinical depression and prescribed medication which calmed him down and helped him to control his temper. Since standing up to him and then joining the Fire Service he had gradually started to treat me with more respect, and he seemed genuinely pleased that I'd achieved something worthwhile. I was nineteen years old and had been training for just three and a half years - which was very quick to get a black belt back then, especially in Kyokushin.

By contrast Pete was really unhappy that I had gone ahead without his permission. I was perplexed. Everyone else was delighted so I couldn't understand what was wrong. Even Stuart, who was my *sempai,* (senior) gladly shook my hand as I lined up in my new place - above him - at the head of the high grade line.

On the first night back, we had an unusually short session. By now the club trained in three separate classes, but everyone was together in the dojo. They all seemed pleased, so obviously I felt really proud that I had brought credit to the club. Pete sat everyone down and brought me to the front. Photographs were taken for the local press. He praised me highly and told the assembled ranks how proud he was of me and how hard I had trained since joining the dojo, passing everybody to get my black belt first. He then calmly told everyone we would now fight ...

What? I thought I'd misheard that. Pete never usually sparred; he'd certainly never sparred with me since I was a beginner. Stuart had once told me he was brilliant, but a serious leg injury had stopped him sparring or competing. I now faced my instructor in front of everyone. I didn't have time to be intimidated and I felt honoured to be demonstrating my skills with a man I looked up to. That notion dissolved immediately when I realised he was taking things very seriously indeed and within seconds I was fighting hard just to stay upright. As I could move well, I kept him at kicking range and landed a few controlled shots. He soon got bored with that, grabbed my gi jacket and punched me full in the face, breaking my nose. As I was dizzy he shouted, 'Stand up - You're a black belt now!' with a really sarcastic edge to his voice. He bowed with a smug smile. I said 'Osu!' through gritted teeth and returned to my place holding my nose to stem the blood. The dojo sat in stunned silence.

This was not the happy and congratulatory occasion I had envisaged, but was the first indication to me that Pete simply could not stand it when anyone crossed him or went against his authority. His wife told me years later that he had laughed about 'spoiling Gary's good looks' when he went home. Not nice. Although I still respected his karate ability, as a man I now saw a different side to his character that I was very uncomfortable with. I continued to train and was given teaching responsibilities immediately, but somehow I already knew my days of training at Leicester were now numbered.

Following Pete's unique welcome back, my next eye-opener as a new black belt was being picked for the BKK under 21 team to fight in the British Karate Control Commission All-Styles Championships in Belle Vue, Manchester. On arrival I was told I couldn't fight without shin pads, so we had a frantic rush around to find some before stepping up to the mat. I was just about to go on when the team coach said, 'Don't forget, if you're losing with ten seconds to go, knock him out!' 'Sorry?' I thought I'd misunderstood, but he repeated the instruction. As this was a 'points' Tournament, the rules specifically forbade landing blows with any force or malice. Despite that, as Kyokushin was promoted as being the strongest, my coach wanted me to deliberately foul my opponent - disqualification being far better than losing, in his opinion. The BKK had a long-running gripe about biased refereeing in this event, so I suppose ethics were long gone by then. This also ignored the fact that my opponent could knock me out if he likewise chose to break the rules, so in that sense proved absolutely nothing.

I refused, fought fair and lost to my faster and technically superior opponent without complaining. Later that day, I saw one non-Kyokushin fighter repeatedly faking being caught by face punches. This Oscar nominated performance subsequently resulted in each of his opponents getting disqualified and taking him as far as the semi-finals. This was remarkably similar to soccer players earning penalties by acting things up and was both cynical and unsporting. I decided on the spot that from now on, I'd focus on the 'knockdown' style.

In knockdown, full contact was allowed to designated target areas, so it required a greater level of personal courage and from where I stood it certainly seemed more honest. Fights were hard and potentially dangerous, but conducted with respect and fair play. That was what I sought, a real challenge where I could test myself out.

Dark Side

It is often quoted that Martial Arts are mainly about character development. My experiences so far with various instructors, a team coach and now even top competitors seemed to be directly at odds with that. Many were complete bastards under the skin. They had all shown a tendency to abuse their skills or ignore the normal codes of conduct as they saw fit, despite all their training and ability. I was to read years later a quote from Vince Lombardi, 'Sport doesn't build character, it reveals it.' Although this was *Budo* (Martial Way) and therefore not strictly sport, I still wondered why I was constantly being urged to use control and follow the rules, while the top dogs didn't seem to care much for either. Perhaps they simply felt themselves above all that.

The Leicester dojo had by now moved to full-time premises above the 'Starflow' garage in

Leicester's Belgrave Gate. The place was a tip when we moved, but everyone mucked in and the experience of painting and renovation built a really good club spirit. At Moat Boys School we had had the run of the huge upstairs gym with a sprung wood floor, perfect for fighting as you could do sweeps and take downs without inflicting serious damage. It also had a downstairs hall with a woodblock floor for more technical instruction. The move to our own dojo was great in some ways. This was right in the 1970's 'Kung-Fu' craze and the club had hundreds of members, but this success now presented new problems. The dojo was only about half the size of the school's upstairs gym. Before long we had twice the membership in a quarter of the space.

Pete's solution was to divide the classes into more specific groups. There were children's classes, ladies' classes, white belt classes, blue and yellow belt classes, green, brown and black belt classes, and even 'stamina' and ladies' keep fit classes. While this made perfect sense economically, it severely restricted the times available. I had a key, so my solution was to come in early to work the bags alone. I then trained in the white belt class, taught the blue and yellow belt class and finally trained again in the green, brown and black belt class. I was always there for four to five hours on training nights, at least twice a week depending on my shifts.

The other change that became immediately apparent was in the fighting. Lots of students crammed into a smaller space made quality sparring difficult to organise. The dojo had a concrete floor with a thin carpet covering, so sweeps were now banned. Niceties like ramming people up to a wall and hammering the body, once a favourite, were first discouraged then banned altogether. The dojo now focused on points fighting rather than organised brawling, and within two years Leicester had won the British WUKO (points) Championships in superb style. For me though I found this very frustrating. I wanted to be really strong, and after fighting in European Summer Camps using the knockdown system, points fighting now left me cold and uninspired. The BKK had by now introduced the knockdown system for black belt competitors at their annual championships and I needed to prepare, but I was constantly being told to 'go easy'. This felt like going backwards.

People starting karate to build their confidence (as I had) may imagine the process as like a winding path meandering up a hill. Weakness at the bottom, with a long steady climb to physical and mental strength at the top. I disagree. In my opinion the process is more like the path of a pendulum. If you imagine this for a moment, picture that the place of strength and courage is dead centre at the lowest point of the arc. If you start from a very weak position, i.e. high up on the 'timid' side, you perhaps naturally then swing *through* this optimal mid-point and across to the dark or 'arrogant' side. If you then get taken down a peg, the pendulum swings back and you become timid again before once more reversing the swing. Each subsequent timid / arrogant swing becomes successively smaller, until eventually the pendulum stops permanently at the mid-point and you are fit, skilful and mentally tough. *You respect everyone yet fear no-one.* This is the mental and physical state we should all strive to reach and for many, this means a lot of very hard work with several disappointments and high points along the way. My guess is that some individuals swing across to the arrogant side and are never corrected or knocked back. They then get stuck at that point, believing they are always right. If so, despite whatever technical skills they may acquire, the mental side of their training hasn't worked and they are still a poor example to others.

Having started as a weak and timid teenager, I got stronger very quickly but unfortunately my 'pendulum' now went right over to the dark side. I trained hard and I sparred hard, and the dojo quickly split into two camps. Half would avoid me at all costs. If we were told to partner up for fighting, they quickly grabbed anyone except me, exactly as I had done years before with Ted Smith. The other half were all bigger and stronger than me or just more vicious. They didn't mind fighting with me and always went very hard. We were constantly being told to go easy, but I didn't care. I was young and hungry for success so I just got stuck in.

We have to accept that many people who train in karate just want a good sweat with no pain, so even the sight of high grades fighting hard and drawing blood makes them nervous and puts them off. For every one that thinks *I want to be that good!* There are probably half a dozen who think, *I hope I never get hit like that!*

As he now had huge bills to pay, Pete was understandably cautious about lost revenue and if anyone quit he wanted to know why. The ethos of training had subtly shifted. When I joined, if you couldn't handle the fighting you left and nobody gave a damn. The onus was on the individual to come up to scratch. Now, if somebody left it was assumed that someone (usually me) had been too hard on them. Before long contact sparring dwindled and almost stopped. I now seemed to be constantly doing basics, kata and 'easy' fighting when I wanted to prepare for knockdown. I had no choice but to look further afield.

Squad Trainings

I had been to lots of courses in London already and really enjoyed them. Stuart had driven me down in his old Reliant three wheeler and the training had always been a lot of fun. Steve Arneil was very charismatic and inspiring. Sensei Brian Fitkin had also been at the first one I attended, along with Sensei Howard Collins who was newly returned from Japan. I watched them both training and was very impressed. They were streets ahead of the rest.

In 1975, the BKK selected a team to travel to Japan for the first World Tournament, with Howard Collins being an automatic choice and Joe Claronino, Billy Walsh and Joe Borg being picked at a black belt course. Training with these top fighters was a huge step up in class. I managed to catch a few people with roundhouse kicks but was quite relieved my name was not called out, as I was smart and honest enough to realise I was still well out of my depth.

It inspired my interest though and I started going to 'squad training' whenever my shifts allowed. They were usually held at Haringey in London with Joe Claronino in charge. The format was roughly the same each time; lots of stamina work, bag work and combinations; followed by many rounds of fighting. On one I found myself facing Glen Sharp. He was a ferocious young fighter who eventually went on to fight in Japan at the Third World Tournament and do really well. We started off at a frantic pace, and more by luck than judgement I swept him as he threw a low kick and followed up with a punch. Unfortunately, he had started to spring up the instant he hit the floor and my 'controlled' punch hit his nose with a sickening crunch. There was a murmur of outrage from everyone watching. His nose was smashed with the bone sticking sideways out of the skin. He was taken off to hospital and the mood turned really ugly. Despite my protestations of no malicious intent, Joe Claronino wisely decided not to call me up to fight again.

Glen was an East Ender. That meant the southerners (most of the squad) loved him. I was a new face from 'Way up North', so they really wanted to beat me up and send me back to Leicester with my tail between my legs. I got out alive and returned home, only for Pete to tell me he'd had a telephone call informing him I wasn't welcome again at the squads; and furthermore if I *did* go again I could expect no quarter. Not the best start to my international ambitions.

In spite of the obvious threat I went again (that stubborn streak over-riding common sense) and had a very rough time. Some grudgingly accepted my willingness to front up, but I don't mind admitting it was one of the scariest things I've ever done. During the long journey down to London my nerves and adrenaline levels hit redline with about 50 miles to go. I rushed to the toilet as soon as I arrived, feeling physically sick with apprehension. The reality was never as bad as I imagined though which was a valuable lesson for the future. Fear - real fear - is an instinctive reaction that prepares the body for combat or escape. This wasn't *real* fear; it was just an uncomfortable reaction to an *imaginary* beating-up. When the fighting started I fought hard but fair. Some tried it on - although Glen himself accepted it was an accident and we got on just fine - but I gave as good as I got. After a few further sessions the animosity cooled and I became a regular member of the squad. I didn't like several of the people there, and I'm damn sure they didn't like me, but in a way this helped me improve far faster than if we'd been good mates. I was to fight several of them in Tournaments in later years, so learning their strengths and weaknesses under pressure was invaluable.

Gashaku!

Most of karate training is indoors. As a lad brought up on fresh air and cycling this was strange at first but of course you adapt and get used to it. The smell of sweat and 'Deep Heat' got stifling sometimes so any chance to train outdoors was welcome. Twice a year most of the dojo jumped into cars and headed off down to Norfolk for a *Gashaku*, or outdoor training weekend. One of the green belts, Cliff Johnson, was a real Arthur Daley type with his fingers in loads of pies. He had a 'mate' that ran a holiday camp (?) which we booked pre- and post-season. To call it a camp was stretching things a bit. In reality it was a motley collection of broken down huts and a few static caravans that were well past their best.

The format was always the same. After work on Friday everyone jumped into cars and drove the 120 miles to the coast. We met in the local pub to take on calories of the liquid kind and later staggered back to the luxury accommodation. As a sempai I usually got to share a caravan, which was bearable but still unpleasant. If I close my eyes I can still remember the smell of damp blankets, piss buckets (the toilet block was about 300 muddy yards away) and biscuits. At least we had a heater. The others shivered all night in their damp huts. At 6:00am we gathered in track suits for a run on the beach, while any wives or girlfriends who'd been lured along on the promise of a romantic weekend away grumbled together and rustled up bacon cobs for breakfast. There was a basics session later on the muddy field, followed by a sandwich lunch and fighting training in the afternoon. It always seemed to rain, so on Saturday evenings we moved on to a local hall for the party / talent show, and then assembled again bleary eyed and hung over at 6:00am on Sunday.

The Sunday beach training was slightly less enthusiastic in this condition, with seagulls being rewarded on occasions as people got rid of their last night's excesses. After the training we had a furious game of 'murderball' - a bit like Rugby with a heavy wet leather medicine ball - which the brown and black belts always seemed to win. After a few closing speeches, we then ran to the cars again Le Mans style and the race back to Leicester was like the Cannonball run, only fiercer and more competitive. I normally grabbed a lift in Cliff's Cortina Lotus, and most times we won in grand style. These were fantastic times as a club, and the shared hardships certainly drew us all together.

Pete had by now started to get involved in charity work. Firemen regularly see horrific injuries at work, so it is perhaps natural that we often support charities, in particular local hospitals and burns units. After one gashaku, some joker said, 'Why don't we run back?' An idea was planted that gradually grew until every year the dojo completed long barefoot runs for charity. The longest I ever took part in was from Hunstanton to Leicester, about 100 miles. Although we ran in relays, we each did about ten miles on public roads and by the end my feet were in bits. Again though, the shared hardship bonded us together. Pete was eventually awarded the British Empire Medal for his charity work, and thoroughly deserved it having organised it all and raised many thousands of pounds.

Demonstrations

The dojo also ran loads of demonstrations, although they didn't always go to plan. These could be anywhere, but the idea was always to support charities and advertise the club. There were too many to recount in detail, but one sticks in my mind for obvious reasons.

We were asked to demonstrate at Western Fire Station at an Open day. Pete was on duty so it fell to me to get things organised. It was to be held outdoors on the rough concrete drill yard. We could do a few basics and maybe a slow kata, but the surface was just horrible so anything more fancy was out of the question in bare feet. I decided breaking would form the majority of what we did. One of the members was a builder and offered to supply the correct materials.

I was at work the night before, and planning what we'd do. One of my watch mates saw me practising and asked what I'd break. 'Blocks,' I replied. I meant thermalite, or cinder blocks which were commonly used to line internal walls. They were quite easy to break three or four at a time, but still looked spectacular. 'What with?' he asked. 'Head butt,' I replied, wondering why he was suddenly so interested. 'Jesus! Are you kidding? How many?' 'Three, maybe four, I'm not sure how many he's got.' He then ran around the station telling everyone. Interest picked up. A book was opened and money changed hands, betting on whether I would break them or knock myself out.

In the morning I got a phone call. The lad bringing the blocks now couldn't make it so I had a frantic ring around to try to get alternative materials. One promised some wood, another assured me he'd got some blocks he could bring. On arrival they were true to their word. We left the stuff in the car boots to keep the place tidy and wandered around the stalls. At the appointed time we got changed and about twelve of us filed out into the yard. We did a brief demo to polite applause, and then laid out a groundsheet for the breaking. I asked the lad to get the wood, and found he'd simply cut up some old floorboards into about 18 inch lengths. Normal wood for Tournaments or demonstrations was piranha pine, 12 x 8 x 1 inch thick. This was horrible dark wood, painted on one side and about 4 inches wide and 18 inches long *along the grain*. I had planned a set up of five people holding boards at various heights and angles to demonstrate a variety of techniques, but could instantly tell that that wouldn't work.

The length of the wood meant it would be springy enough to take all the force out of the blow, and the direction of grain meant it couldn't be snapped. The best I could hope for would be a messy tearing break with loads of splinters. As half my shift had come up to watch I had to do something, so for lack of any other idea I stacked about 5 together to make them more rigid and smashed them with an elbow strike. They broke, but not cleanly. The crowd grew restless and started to drift away... 'Ladies and Gentlemen!' boomed the PA system. 'Gary Chamberlain, a Fireman from Central Fire Station, will now break blocks ... With his head!'

The crowd murmured and turned back. The blocks arrived and to my horror I saw they were the wrong type of blocks. These were the type used for external load bearing walls, and made from rough grit and concrete. To make things even worse they were muddy and soaking wet. I really wished the ground would open up and swallow me. My workmates were by now grinning like Cheshire cats. No-one likes to have their courage questioned and in the Fire Brigade it is essential to trust the moral fibre of anyone you are expected to go into danger with. Bottling out was therefore not an option. With this in mind I pushed common sense and self-preservation to one side and grimly set the blocks up. 'Where the hell did you get these from?' I hissed. 'Under me dad's shed,' he replied. 'You TWAT! How the hell am I supposed to break these? I can hardly lift them they're so bleedin' wet.' 'Dunno... Sorry.'

I stood back and bowed to the crowd, then measured the distance for a head butt onto two blocks balanced precariously on supports with a slight gap in between. The crowd fell silent and waited with baited breath. Adrenaline kicked in and with a huge 'Sheeeria!' I dropped my head and smashed through them. Sparks flew everywhere inside my skull and I went blind for a few seconds. As my sight cleared I saw two broken blocks and heard applause, quickly followed by screaming from the children and shouting from the adults. Confused, I stood up and spun around, noticing a strange red mist following me. A woman swooned and just narrowly caught on to someone before she fell. I felt strange sticky warmth pouring down my head.

A Fireman rushed up, threw a towel over me and ushered me away. On going into the toilets I saw just above the hairline a gaping split running across the crown of my head and oozing blood. I was taken to the local Hospital for six stitches and given a sick note for a week. On returning to work my boss was not impressed, but my shift mates were delighted. They had taken bets with Firemen from other stations and made a small fortune. It was nice to know they had faith in me.

Over the years I broke ice, wood, bricks, tiles, blocks, bottles and baseball bats; but from that day onwards I always took my own carefully selected materials.

Sensei Tatsuo Nakamura

In my opinion - looking back - one of the best moves ever by the BKK was to employ a Japanese instructor. This was controversial at the time, as legendary home-grown talents like Howard Collins and Brian Fitkin had been sidelined and were now teaching overseas. Many doubted what Tatsuo Nakamura; a small Japanese 4th Dan would be able to improve. After all, the BKK was by now long established and was running huge successful events. British fighters fought well all over the world, and Steve Arneil had recently coached the first non-Japanese team to win the WUKO (points) World Championships. In my opinion, speaking as an ambitious young fighter, I wanted to learn all I could about the knockdown style, and as Tatsuo was from the *Honbu* (headquarters) and had fought in the All-Japan Tournament I knew he obviously had a lot to teach. He was to be based in the south of England, but would travel around the country by arrangement with local instructors. I travelled down expectantly to a course where he was to be formally introduced.

The venue was packed, probably more out of curiosity than anything else, and when Tatsuo came in he looked quite frail. I glanced at some of the seasoned British fighters, some of whom were huge hairy men with hands like crane buckets. I honestly wondered how this small man would measure up. Steve Arneil introduced him, but by his tone and general demeanour I guessed he wasn't delighted about this whole arrangement. I doubt he felt upstaged, but he probably also wondered what this young man could bring to the table. Tatsuo then took the warm-up and was impressively flexible. He then showed some combinations, which had everyone open mouthed. Most combinations practised previously were a collection of techniques with various points of focus, but his just *flowed.* His kicks were fantastic, but the speed and sheer grace he moved with was like comparing a thoroughbred to Shire horses. We could tell straight away that this was an extremely effective way of moving. Economical and very, very fast. After about an hour Steve Arneil brought him to the front and asked him who he'd like to fight with. He flashed a smile, showing a row of gold teeth. I turned to the man next to me and whispered, 'I'd hate to fight the man that knocked *his* teeth out.' He grinned back. Then came a shock. 'Gary,' he said, flashing his teeth.

What? Why me? He doesn't even know me! Seared through my mind. To my relief Gary Bufton, a big Welshman, stood up. Gary had trained in Japan a few years before so Tatsuo already knew him. He was a PE teacher, big and strong, so we settled down to see what happened. We were not disappointed. Despite being very gentle, this much smaller fighter completely outclassed him. It was incredible to behold, almost like watching an F1 car racing a Land Rover. Gary sat down smiling and shaking his head. He was no slouch but had been totally outclassed. A few more stepped up and Tatsuo gently kicked them all in the face whenever he felt like it, while skilfully avoiding everything they threw back in return. This was a revelation. Until then my fighting was all about getting in range and throwing bombs. He changed my whole way of thinking in about 10 minutes.

England Team

In 1976 at age 20 I entered the first ever BKK Open Knockdown Tournament at Crystal Palace. This was openweight and for black belts only. The only real coaching I got was from Stuart, who had gamely helped out despite the fact that neither of us really knew what the best tactics were. In truth, apart from the four who had fought in Japan the previous year it was a huge learning curve for everyone.

I felt great leading up to it but things didn't go to plan. In that first year, we had to break wood before being allowed to fight - a minimum of three one inch boards. I was 100% sure I could do this, having previously done it on numerous occasions. In the event I lined up, hit them hard, and looked down in disbelief when there was a huge thud but no crack. I had failed the break. More boards were quickly stacked up, but although it only took seconds my knuckles were already swelling up alarmingly. Cautious not to damage them further before I even fought I switched hands with similar results. Thank you and sit down. I was gutted. My agony was made worse by the fact the points championships was held on the same day and the Leicester team won in superb style. At least that took the pressure off me a little.

Undeterred, I entered the next year. This was now divided into Light (under 75kg) and Heavyweight (over 75kg) categories. The minimum boards had been reduced to two, but to blow the ghost away from the last time I broke three with a punch just to prove to myself that what happened had been a fluke. I had a bye in the first round so was already in the last 16. I then broke three boards with *shuto* (the famous karate chop) before being called up to fight.

My opponent was Joe Borg, a veteran from the first World Tournament. He was not great technically but was older and wiser and really tough. I hit him with everything I'd got, but after two minutes neither of us had scored. The judges signalled a draw which gave us a further round, so I must have been doing OK. In the second round though he came to life, dropping me with a body punch for a half-point score and taking himself through to the quarter finals.

I sat down to handshakes and backslapping from the Leicester supporters and felt I'd acquitted myself quite well. Instead of relaxing, I then noted down every scoring technique throughout the day so I could better understand what worked and what simply looked good. Shihans Nakamura and Oyama were also there and gave a fantastic demonstration that climaxed with one catching a razor sharp Samurai sword. Steve Arneil was promoted to 'Shihan' to a standing ovation that capped off a great day. The Shihans then got drunk together in the bar with everyone giving them a wide berth, especially the nervous security staff.

I had continued with the squads, where the fighting style had now improved dramatically after everyone had witnessed for themselves the most effective techniques. To my delight, in 1978 I was selected to fight in the England Heavyweight team at the first European Championships, to be held in the 10,000 capacity Wembley Arena. I immediately rang my parents to offer to get some tickets but my father just wasn't interested. To him the purpose of unarmed combat was simply to close with the enemy and despatch them as quickly as possible. The idea of fair play and rules meant it was just a game to him, and with typical scorn he just remarked that it was a long way to travel as he couldn't see me getting very far. I decided on the spot I'd be the Champion one day if it killed me just to prove him wrong. *(He later claimed that he was just using reverse psychology - it certainly worked.)*

On the day I felt great, took a good breakfast and walked to the dojo in good spirits. The club had bus loads of people going down to support me, and it suddenly hit me that I carried the hopes of the whole club squarely on my shoulders. My nerves started in earnest. I wasn't afraid of getting hurt, but the thought of letting people down who had given up a day and bought tickets started to eat away at me. On arrival I wandered across to the judges table and glanced at the draw sheet. *My heart sank.* My first opponent was Howard Collins. A feeling of abject helplessness briefly engulfed me. Howard Collins was an iron man who had come second in the 1972 All-Japan Tournament and completed the legendary 100 man kumite in Japan. I was a nervous 22 year old, fit and quite skilful but in other ways still wet behind the ears. I wasn't afraid of him, far from it. In the previous two years he had won the British Open with superb sweeps and takedowns, so I didn't visualise him smashing me up, but rather scoring in some relatively painless but embarrassing way. Others fighters there were far scarier as they seemed to have an unhealthy interested in beating up their opponents rather than skilfully scoring points.

My nerves were more about the very real prospect of looking a chump. Sports stars often talk today of 'imposter syndrome', where they go out to compete and suddenly have a loss of confidence, thinking, *I shouldn't be here - I'm not good enough and I'll be exposed.* I had never even heard of that but I had it - big style. Despite that, as we were called up I just thought, *Stuff it, I'm here now so I'll give it my best shot.* To prepare I had spent hours low kicking a heavy bag as my notes confirmed lots of fights were decided that way, so on *'Hajime!'* (begin) I got on with it. I connected with several good shots but they had no noticeable effect, so I switched to high kicks and to my surprise (and the crowd's) I got through to the face, but without enough power to knock him down. He became a bit more serious now, and with a few seconds to go in the first round he caught me with his trademark sweep to score. Fight over. On returning from the mat the rest of the team crowded round and they all told me I'd done really well. When I watched the tape later I had indeed put up a pretty good show, but inside I burned with frustration. My father had been right. I hadn't got very far and I was now desperate to achieve something worthy of respect and to prove my combat, rather than technical ability.

England Team 1978. 1st European Championships at Wembley Arena.

Back row: Roy Banton, Julian Williams, Barry West, Bernard Creton, GC, Jeff Whybrow

Front: Alan McVicar, Glen Sharp, Lorne Horsford, Graham Sauvarin (RIP), Lloyd Payne, Adrian Clamp

30 Fights

The Summer Camps had by now been moved to Exeter University. The Japanese Shihans were no longer asked over and Steve Arneil headed the team of Instructors. Steve Arneil always had charisma by the bucket load and everyone responded well to his leadership. The training was tough. Without the ominous presence of the stick wielders, people tried because they wanted to and in my opinion were all the better for it. We had a few hard days, including Joe Claronino's merciless early morning conditioning training that basically just ruined your legs for the whole day. On one day we were all told to assemble in the main sports hall for kumite. A few had asked to attempt their 30, 40 and 50 fights. '40' was for 2nd Dans and '50' for 3rd Dans. As I was still 1st Dan I stuck my name down under '30'. I hadn't trained for it specifically, but knew I was in good shape so thought I'd have a go. The rules were as per knockdown but without heavy contact on the low kicks. Each fight lasted one and a half minutes, and you could quit any time by simply indicating you'd had enough.

Needless to say that didn't enter my mind. Some of my opponents were good, while others gave a brief respite and allowed me to catch my breath. In truth some of the opponents were just there to make up the numbers, and I found myself getting mad as they weren't going hard enough. The test took about an hour, and while it was quite hard, especially the last ten, I honestly never considered quitting. By the end I was tired, but immediately went over to support the ones who were carrying on to '40' and then '50'. It became obvious that several of the high grades didn't want anyone passing their '50'. Some were really wading in but the candidates stuck it out and earned everyone's respect. In later years anyone was allowed to attempt higher numbers at any level, so I often regret not being allowed to carry on for more. I was very fit and skilful so believe in my heart I could have kept pressing on.

I returned to Leicester dojo quite happy with my 30 kumite certificate, but was soon sad to hear that Stuart had decided to stop training. I never found out why but it was a real loss to me. While Pete had built up the numbers, Stuart had given me lots of extra coaching and sound advice. His decision to stop, although it was his personal choice, was a real loss to the club and many of us felt the same way.

Second Dan

I next focussed on taking my 2nd Dan in the September. Despite saying before that grades didn't interest him; Pete had applied for and later passed his 2nd Dan once I got my 1st Dan. He also now insisted on being called Sempai Kisby during training, whereas before 'Pete' had been just fine. To be fair this was decreed from above, rather than just by his own ego. Getting my black belt had been like the first four minute mile at Leicester. There were lots of good brown belts there, many stronger than me, but it just needed someone to burst through that psychological barrier and pass to get them all motivated. Within three years many more had succeeded, so now I wanted to stay in front. Training at Leicester was always very technical. Pete was very precise when instructing and the general standard was high. I had hoped he would now give me extra coaching, but apart from one kata session in the hall at Central Fire

Station he simply said, 'You'll be fine.'

That was hardly reassuring as the tests were notoriously difficult. At a previous one the cream of British Kyokushinkai had gathered and done their best, only for Steve Arneil to stop the test after 30 minutes to say, 'Thank you Gentlemen. We have seen enough. This is not the standard we require.' Quite a few had thrown their toys out the pram and were never seen again. This made me all the more keen to prepare properly.

The BKK syllabus had lists of techniques required at each level. These had to be demonstrated in a variety of stances and combinations. Precision and power was required, and any sloppiness at all was enough reason to fail. Kata obviously had to be spot on. The examiners sat at a high table, and each watched the candidates like a hawk. Pete was one of the examiners. Due to numbers, the brown belts attempting black belt went in first and many were failed. Those attempting 2nd Dan then went in and none of us were very optimistic.

The test was unusually brief. A little over an hour of basics in various stances then kata in a group and individually. The examiners just sat impassively taking notes. No fighting, no combinations, no breaking, and then suddenly Steve Arneil stood up and thanked us and we were told to wait outside. We sat in the changing rooms thinking the whole day had been a waste of time. After 15 minutes we went back in to hear the verdict. I had passed, but with the proviso that I must, 'Help Peter.' (?) and tidy up my kata. I was very disappointed. I'd rather have failed than be passed with strings attached. Pete rubbed it in a bit on the way back, explaining that the rest of the panel had wanted to hold me back but he had fought hard for me. To this day I don't know if that was true or was just said to keep me in my place and make me feel obligated.

True to form, Pete soon passed his 3rd Dan - ever anxious to be one step in front - and then insisted on being addressed as Sensei. I now had two people that I really wanted to surpass. I wanted to be technically better than Pete and to be far tougher - mentally and physically - than my father had been in his prime, although with rather more self-control.

Stockholms Karate Kai

Sensei (now Shihan) Brian Fitkin was awesome. He had won the World Championship as part of the British All-Styles team in 1975, and his skill and timing were second to none. He was a regular visitor to the BKK Summer Camp in Exeter each year. Pete rated him above all others as he had been taught by him up to black belt, as Brian had travelled up to Leicester each week to teach. Sadly this finished before I joined and he had later moved to Stockholm.

I mentioned one day I'd love to go there, and Pete immediately said, 'Why not?' He offered to give me a letter of introduction, which was nice of him but seemed a little unnecessary as we had already met on Summer Camps. I wrote to enquire, (this is long before email) and Brian agreed I could come over. I didn't know what to expect. I knew several BKK black belts had gone over and come back very humble. Even Bernard

Creton, a superb technician with a reputation for hard fighting, had got no change at all out of Brian but had come back quietly, licking his wounds.

In the Fire Service leave is allocated in blocks to maintain manning levels. My next block was in December, not the best time to be travelling to Scandinavia as the temperature was regularly minus 30°C at that time of year. I was keen to go though so pushed ahead. Brian had previously brought a few of his students to England to compete and they always looked superb, so I just thought *even if it's tough, it'll be well worth it.* On the night before going, Pete gave me his letter in a sealed envelope. I've often wondered over the years what he put, but I'll take a guess that 'needs taking down a peg or two' featured in there somewhere. That's not to say Brian would have been swayed by that, he was his own man and would doubtless have decided for himself.

I duly arrived in Stockholm, a wonderful place aptly described as 'The Venice of the North'. Desperately cold of course, but as a country lad I was not well travelled so it was a great place to visit. Brian picked me up at the coach station and took me to the dojo, where the annual party was already in full swing. I was given a room to use and gladly joined in the festivities. As we finished up he asked whether I was fit. I replied reasonably so, and mentioned I trained in every class at Leicester so would like to do the same in Stockholm. He shot me a glance and quietly suggested that I might need all my stamina for the high grade class alone. A shiver of nerves ran through me, as I realised this was no holiday, not by a long way. He then said he'd be at the dojo the next day to give me a private session, passed me some keys and left. I slept fitfully, thinking the worst.

The next day some students came in early to clean up, and later Brian arrived. He seemed happy enough and we changed for training. Stockholms Karate Kai main dojo was on the top floor and was a really beautiful place, with a lovely smooth wooden floor and mirrors all along one wall adding to the atmosphere. We bowed and warmed up and then put on pads. He pulled out some old bag gloves and casually mentioned he liked to wear them when sparring as then he didn't have to control face punches so much ...

My backside started to clench hard enough to crack a nut. *What?* I had been focussing on knockdown training where face punches were illegal. I now stood miles from home about to face a World Champion who seemed pretty damned casual about punching me in the face. Suddenly this seemed like a nightmare, but with *'Hajime!'* It got far, far worse. One of the oldest tricks in the book is to feint with a right front kick, drawing the opponents left guard hand down and then use the momentum of the returning leg to throw in a long right punch over the lowered guard. I saw it coming as if in slow-motion but was just mesmerised. It hit me square on the nose, which having been broken before now gave a loud internal crack and firework display and started pouring with blood. This was the *first* punch of the *first* session on the *first* day. *Only eleven long days to go,* I thought grimly.

He seemed genuinely sorry, and re-set my septum on the spot. This was unpleasant but it later remained straighter than before so he did a good job. We then carried on sparring, but he now avoided the face altogether and focused instead on sweeps. Anyone who saw him at Summer Camps in the 1970s will remember his sweeps. He had feet like shovels and could take anyone down from impossible angles no matter what kick they threw. We continued like this for almost an hour. I had good kicks and had recently caught Howard Collins full in the face, but I couldn't get near him. No matter what I did he swept me and I landed heavily on my side, back, elbow, knee, face or just whatever happened to hit the ground first. I have never been so outclassed, before or since. The man was incredible.

After a while though, just getting up off the floor became a real struggle. My lower legs were quite skinny and a worrying loss of sensation was causing me real concern. Eventually, I asked if we could stop. 'Sure,' he said, turned on his heel and walked straight out of the dojo. I felt like a dog. After a few moments I went to the changing rooms and apologised, but quite genuinely argued that since I was to be there for twelve days I wanted to be in a fit state to continue training past the first session. He seemed unmoved, but as I took off my gi bottoms and limped into the shower he saw my shins and calf muscles were covered in ugly raised lumps. 'Oh yes, it is quite bad isn't it,' was his only comment, to be followed a few moments later by, 'but we were going to stop soon anyway.'

I felt really bad. Brian was one of those special people for whom quitting was never an option. I've met a few like him over the years - most of them ex military - who could think on their feet no matter how exhausted they were and not even consider giving up. I wanted that mindset and was determined to find it in the future. My nose hurt as much as my legs, but my pride hurt far more. Years later, Lance Armstrong summed this up with his famous quote, 'Pain is temporary, quitting lasts forever.' I made a solemn promise to myself to do better from now on. This was a pivotal moment, where the desire to keep going now massively overtook mere physical discomfort.

It took a while before I gradually accepted that no-one who had gone to Sweden had found it easy, and as I had lasted almost an hour with a man of his capabilities I had in reality done quite well. The whole point of the pressure that was so expertly applied was to show me how much I could take. It was not done maliciously, but to take me further out of my comfort zone than ever before. When you experience this type of training, you have to focus, dig deep and keep trying for as long as possible - pushing far past your 'limits,' which most of the time are mental, not physical. I felt regret about stopping - I still do - but as I had now fought longer and harder against a far tougher opponent than I had ever done previously, squad trainings and Tournaments later paled by comparison. We had another hour of sparring later in the week, thankfully this time in a matted dojo, and despite being winded after body punches, I persevered and got through it so my self-belief started to grow. This is exactly what he set out to give me, and in the longer term the experience did me a tremendous amount of good.

The rest of the trip was fantastic. Training in the

advanced class was superb, and everyone made me welcome and helped a lot. At Leicester I was one of the biggest, in Stockholm one of the smallest. Despite that, I still struggled to keep up with the sheer speed and intensity of the class. Training in Stockholm that winter remains one of my best karate experiences. It was the start of growing confidence and really paid off later. I found a lot out about myself. I didn't like it when I gave up, and immediately set about putting things right. This didn't happen overnight, but was well worth it in the end.

Great Britain Team

In 1979 I fought again in the heavyweights. I was 23 and raring to go. The BKK was about to select a team to go to the second World Tournament, and we were told the top four would be seriously considered. I got through the first two rounds easily and felt really strong. In the last eight I faced a non-Kyokushin stylist by the name of Charles White. He had scraped through his earlier fights and appeared to be limping. Any performance nerves from earlier in the day were by now gone and I knew I could blow him away. I decided to work on his injured leg and then knock him down when his hands dropped, a strategy I had used effectively before and had no reason to doubt.

In the event he was a tough customer who gamely kept moving forwards and despite being in pain got a draw after the first two minutes. This meant a two minute extension but I didn't care, I was fit enough to do this all day. He was limping badly by now so I just continued to smash away at his legs. A fighter rarely hears much from the crowd, but for some reason I heard 'Knock him out! Knock him out!' being chanted by the Leicester crowd. *Okay,* I thought, *if that's what you want.* I set him up for the high kick, swinging my leg in a huge arc ... and felt a sharp pain in my rib. He knew my plan; timing his under punch perfectly and tipping me off balance. I got up immediately. I was winded but went straight back to work. I was now half a point down and time was short. Charles covered up like a tortoise and took everything, but he simply would *not* go down.

I had lost in the stupidest fashion imaginable. Every judge said afterwards they'd already got their flags ready and I would have won 5:0 on a judge's decision, but I'd blown it by trying to put on a show. Another harsh lesson: 'Effective' always looks good, while 'looking good' is not always effective. I shook my head in shock and disbelief. If they're honest, few fighters mind losing to a worthy opponent, but although Charles was tough he just hadn't done anything - except for one perfectly timed punch. I felt absolutely gutted. Charles then went on to fight Bernard Creton in the semi-final. After watching me, Bernard was smart enough to keep his kicks zeroed in on his legs and not try for the knockout, winning on a judge's decision.

Charles was a really tough bloke and I shook his hand and congratulated him. He took tremendous punishment and had certainly performed well above the norm on the basis of his extraordinary courage. As I left the Crystal Palace Arena that evening, Joe Claronino beckoned me over. He was a man of few words. I expected some laconic yet useful advice. 'You really fucked that up,' was all he said. *Thanks Joe, I hadn't realised*.

The team selected for Japan was Howard Collins - automatically - as he had won easily in the previous three years and was vastly experienced; along with the Tournament's highest placed heavyweight fighters. Jeff Whybrow (1st place) Bernard Creton (2nd place) and Alwyn Heath (Joint 3rd) Charles had taken 'my' third place. Howard Collins went to New York to prepare, but the rest of the team would be training full-time before leaving at Leicester dojo. I was invited to go along to make up a four for sparring and partner work. After fighting Brian Fitkin, I wasn't over-awed by any of them. Jeff was very stylish. Bernard was ruthless. He and I had previously clashed at a Summer Camp where he had tried to work me over and I had kicked him full in the mouth. After that he had backed off a bit, but I fully expected him to try and sharpen his teeth on me over the coming week and I was determined to take no shit. Alwyn was just gritty, not flash in any way but absolutely dogged. I hoped that if anyone got injured in the build-up I might be asked go in their place, but it was not to be. The whole squad fought really well and did the BKK proud. Congratulations to them all.

Later that year the BKK sent what was in effect a 'B' team to Switzerland for a four way match between Great Britain, Switzerland, Belgium and Holland. At the selection I had fought Roy Banton, Joe Claronino's top student and to my mind had had the measure of him. He complained bitterly later that I had fouled him and to my disgust was made team Captain over me. Great Britain drew Holland first and I faced Nico Gordeau. We had a good hard fight which ended in a draw, which was permissible in team events. I was pleased as he outweighed me by about 15 kilos so holding him to a draw was still a credible result. The team lost but we had all also been entered in the individual events. Sadly, I had broken my hand somehow and the doctor ordered me to hospital, where a full plaster cast stopped any ideas of competing any further.

Getting Personal

In 1980 I was again picked for the England team, this time in a three way match against Holland and Sweden to be held at the Welsh Open Tournament. We fought Holland first, and this time I found myself against Gerard Gordeau, Nico's brother. Gerard was taller and heavier than me, but again I forced a draw, even managing to hook a hand behind his neck (legal at the time) and put a knee kick hard into his face. This tapped his claret, but to his credit he stayed on his feet so I didn't score. He was a real warrior and later fought with distinction in the UFC.

In the next round against Sweden, I now fought Kurt Pettersson, who was about 6'7" tall although not particularly heavy. He was long limbed and awkward though, so I found it difficult to get into effective range. In desperation I put *both* hands behind his neck, pulled him forwards and again used the knee, but this time I was judged to have *grabbed* rather than *hooked* and was disqualified. In truth the difference between the two was largely a matter of the referee's interpretation and viewpoint, but the disqualification stood and I obviously felt bad about letting the team down.

The annual Tournament was now coming up fast, and despite breaking my wrist a few weeks earlier it had healed well and I was keen enough to enter. I always fought at heavyweight, which was anything over 80 kilograms. I usually weighed in at about 84, which often made me one of the smaller fighters in the category. Many of the Europeans, especially the Dutch and Swedish were often several inches taller and a lot heavier. As I had fought against bigger men in team matches I felt confident enough. The rules stated that for individual matches if the fight was drawn after 4 minutes the lighter man won, so being lighter sometimes became an advantage.

This did reflect a grave error in my tactical thinking though. My training focused a lot on stamina work and lactate tolerance. I could last all day at a high work rate, but against much bigger opponents where head kicks were more difficult to land I had to focus on the body and legs. I found I was not quite powerful enough to be sure of knocking them down.

A few years previously there had been an ugly split at the Leicester dojo. Lee Morris, a likeable enough chap, had been put in the unlucky position of addressing a few grievances from some of the members. One of the malcontents was Vince Halliday, an extremely powerful man who had once considered professional boxing. He had punches that would drop a donkey and was in superb physical shape. At a crisis meeting at the dojo, he and I clashed and had to be separated or would have got into it on the spot. The meeting dissolved and Lee started his own dojo at Melton Mowbray with Vince as his right hand man. Now, four years later, after breezing through the early rounds again to reach the last eight, I faced him across the mat.

One of my friends at work had told me something a few months earlier that had rather unsettled me. Vince worked as a mechanic at the local Gas Board. My friend also worked there part-time and had asked me why Vince had my picture placed prominently on display above his bench. *What?* I thought, *that's spooky.* I tried to sound calm about it, but as Vince didn't appear to respect me and I'm equally sure he didn't find me attractive, I could only assume this provided constant motivation to train hard in the hope of tearing me to pieces at the first available opportunity. I had fought dozens of hard fights by now at squads, Camps and Tournaments, not to mention hundreds at the dojo and never taken anything *that* personally. I always trained hard and tried my best on the day, but if someone beat me I congratulated them, shook their hand and often as not bought them a beer afterwards.

Vince glared at me. Before my fights I now reminded myself that against Brian Fitkin I had dragged myself up off the floor probably a hundred times over nearly an hour. No matter what happened here in four minutes it could never be that hard, so by that yardstick alone I had nothing to worry about, so long as I stayed sharp and aggressive. Looking into the apparent hatred in his eyes though I felt this was far more serious to him than respectful combat sport. I began to think *we'd be better off taking this outside, as at least then we won't have rules to worry about.* Using my father's brutal techniques and unsporting military ethics now seemed far more appealing, but by now we were bowing and about to get started.

On 'Hajime!' We circled a little, both wary of silly mistakes. He was slightly shorter than me but much more powerful, so I'm sure he watched for my kicks while I knew he was a big puncher so kept a tight guard. I tried a probing front kick and BANG, a huge punch hit me much harder than I expected. We moved again, I feinted a roundhouse kick, BANG, he caught me again. My strategy was playing straight into his hands. To tire people out and break their spirit I usually used low kicks, but he waited and counter punched superbly. Inevitably he found a way through and caught me so hard I dropped to one knee gasping for air. I heard the count reach five but couldn't even breathe. He had beaten me by a full point, and now smiled and held out his hand. Maybe I had misjudged his mood - who knows? I met him several times again over the years and we got on just fine. For now though, I had once again reached the last eight from a pool of thirty two and gone home empty handed. This was becoming a habit that I was keen to put right.

The next day an x-ray confirmed a rib fracture and I was pissing blood, so on medical advice I took a week off before returning to light training. No-one called me to find out how I was, and I found out later that the dojo high grades had held a meeting in my absence where Pete had accused me of cowardice. He also boasted, 'That punch wouldn't have put me down,' which stung me to the core.

Anyone lacking courage and self-belief doesn't enter Knockdown Tournaments, let alone fight year after year both at home and abroad against the best opponents they can find. Sure, I had lost, but most of my critics had sat and watched rather than test themselves. I had stepped up to the mark and fought, which to my mind deserved credit regardless of the result on the day. When all's said and done this was combat sport, not life and death, so questioning my courage - which was regularly tested at work and had always held up - was insulting. I took this very hard. I was seething and thought *stuff what they think, they never even enter, let alone win.* I now felt cold fury driving me on.

Doorman

Pete now joined my father at the head of my imaginary 'Must prove wrong' list. In some ways they were very similar. In my father's case there had been good times marred by his temper and scornful remarks. In Pete's case there was a lot of good advice and technical instruction, but for some reason he seemed to question my character and put me down verbally more than any other student. I was now fiercely determined to prove them both wrong. How would I do this? Winning the British Open Knockdown Championships seemed like a good start.

For now though I relaxed a bit. I continued to train regularly but my heart wasn't really in it. I was also sick of teaching night after night for free, and in particular, running lucrative 'pre-grading' courses and such like for just a cursory, 'Thank you.' In lieu of any payment I had previously enjoyed the use of the club minibus and had a dojo key so I could train any time, but for some unknown reason these were now both withdrawn. I also had things to sort out domestically. I had been house-sitting for a friend for a few months, but as he was now getting married I had to move out. I was fed up renting flats so decided to buy a small cottage of my own in a nice local village. Although it only cost £13,250, I didn't have the deposit which Building Societies required at the time. I needed more cash.

One of the Leicester students was working a door and casually mentioned he could find me some work if I was interested, as the nightclub he worked at was expanding and needed more staff. I jumped at the chance. I had been going to nightclubs for years and the bouncers always looked bored. I thought it would be an easy ride, so I bought a dinner jacket and bow tie and got the biggest shock of my life.

Any new nightclub took a while to settle. Fights were dealt with harshly until the club enjoyed a 'safe' reputation and 'normal' people felt confident to go there, relax and enjoy themselves. Until then various unsavoury characters tried it on. British nightclubs at the time stopped nice people on the door if they weren't wearing a tie, but let scumbags in if they were wearing one. Once inside, they then gave them a deadly weapon - a beer glass or bottle. If trouble started these were often thrown at high velocity and if a fight was not stopped immediately innocent people could get badly cut by flying glass. More than once I held a young person's face together outside while waiting for an ambulance, which hardened my attitude somewhat towards troublemakers.

My early fights on the door were a very steep learning curve. The knockdown fighting stance popular at the time was to hold the hands high but *away* from the face. As we also held the head up (great for knockdown - harder to kick it way up there) it was like putting a cabbage on a stick and asking people to throw beer glasses at it. Very unpleasant. It was hard to kick effectively on a beer soaked carpet or flight of stairs. Close proximity often meant being grabbed and attacked with glasses or bottles so having no grappling experience I had to learn fast.

Standard procedure quickly became lowering the stance and keeping the guard tight. Then getting in close and grabbing anything - clothes, hair or skin - to pull them onto head butts and get them off balance. Next, bending them forwards so they couldn't lash out and kneeing them hard in the face if they kept struggling. In this position they were then pushed head first through the nearest fire exit which was quickly closed behind them. I'd love to say I then calmly straightened my tie like James Bond, but in truth the adrenaline spike usually left me trying hard not to show the other doormen I was shaking.

I did this for a few months at two different establishments, and probably had half a dozen incidents every week. In this sense it was not unlike the Fire Brigade, periods of relative boredom followed by flashes of dangerous activity. I never felt scared. Dealing with nightclub fights required an instant response, allowing no time for fear and paralysis to take hold. I had been far more nervous in my first few Tournaments, where despite rules, a referee and no sharp weapons, sitting around all day waiting to compete had given me ample opportunity to imagine my biggest fear - letting other people down.

Martial Artists who work on doors are often vilified by others as somehow guilty of violating the guiding principle of *'Karate ni sente nashi'* which is usually translated as 'No first attack in karate.' My own interpretation is 'Don't cause trouble' which I still abide by today. I never gave anyone a good hiding unless they really deserved it, but I must admit if I saw someone throwing glasses they soon wished they'd not bothered. Although some may question the ethics of using karate skills aggressively, in these situations doing nothing would have been far worse as many others could have been hurt. Whenever possible I always tried to act with restraint, steering people out instead of throwing them out. One of the older doormen shook his head at this. 'If you put someone out make sure you hurt them. Run them into a wall or something.' 'Why?' I asked. 'Because then they're scared to come back. If you show them up they'll want revenge, but if they wake up in a lot of pain they won't bother.'

This came true in tragic fashion one night when I was attacked with murderous intent by someone I had 'shown up'. As he was armed I had to hit him so hard he nearly died. The police locked me up overnight 'for my own protection' but thankfully his girlfriend admitted that he had planned to cut me up. This confirmed what I said, that I had only acted in self-defence. I was released without charge, although the custody officer promised, 'We'll get you next time.'

Needless to say I was very relieved he recovered, and at that point decided the odds of survival long term without serious injury or prison were fairly poor and decided to call it a day. A criminal record would have ended my Fire Service career and for the money - although it was good - it just wasn't worth the risk. Years later, I helped out on another door and was disturbed to find no beer and violence, but instead very young kids taking hard drugs in the toilets - hardly an improvement. I've never been to a nightclub since.

Getting Stronger

At the last year's Tournament I had been blown away. Vince had overpowered me - mentally and physically. If I wanted to win, which I did desperately, I now had to power up and get more intense. Most of my training thus far had been more about stamina. I spent hours at the dojo, but to build real strength you have to train against resistance. This forces your central nervous system to adapt and recruit more muscle fibres. Clearly, I wasn't doing that enough in the dojo. I did hundreds of press-ups, sit-ups and squats, but that had only taken my strength so far and was now only training my local muscular endurance. Maximum strength is often affected by genetics and as I was tall and long limbed that didn't help. Specific training was needed.

I knew little then about how the body works, so the sensible thing to do was seek expert advice.

Edwin Brown, or 'Max' as he was known, was a Leicester dojo brown belt and the strongest man I knew. He had seen me lose to Vince, and was keen to help. He suggested I train with him at 'Sugars Gym', a local bodybuilding emporium run by a Mr Great Britain finalist and local strongman by the name of Dennis Christopher. I turned up feeling like a man and left feeling like a little boy. Up until then I had only used light bars for circuit training and of course carried kit regularly at work without too much trouble. In resistance training terms though, I was disappointingly weak.

We started on the bench press. Max put about 80 kilograms on the bar and pumped out 25 repetitions as a warm-up. I got under the bar and couldn't lift it. He took 10 off. No; still too heavy. Down to 60, and I now managed about 5 reps. My arms were shaking but the bar just wouldn't move. He looked at me and gently shook his head. I don't know what he thought, but as he benched about 150 easily, training with me meant an awful lot of changing plates. I was quite strong with my legs, perhaps surprisingly so as they were still long and thin, but my upper body work was disappointing. To Max's credit he never moaned, and sorted out a program to help me get stronger. We trained together regularly and in the build up to the Tournament he pushed my strength levels right up. I owe him a lot. I'm not saying this made me win, but the extra confidence gained by getting stronger all added into the mix.

Not knowing anything about rest and recovery, I just carried on my running and dojo training as normal. I had always eaten a lot - my nickname years earlier had been 'dustbin', but suddenly there wasn't enough food in the world to fill me up. I started to fill out nicely but often felt absolutely exhausted. At about this time, I also saw a spectacular demonstration of real power that later changed my way of training still further. The downstairs gym at the Fire Station had some free weights and an old leather punchbag. I was bored one night and wandered downstairs to find 'Ginger' Allen working out. He was from another station and was heavily into weightlifting, as distinct from bodybuilding although as yet I didn't know the difference. He looked quite ponderous as he single-arm deadlifted an enormous bar with so much weight on it, it literally bent in the middle. He had a strange build, with huge legs, a thick waist and sloping shoulders, and looked positively old-school and unathletic compared to the fine specimens at Sugars Gym.

I started whacking the bag about, which was heavy and solid. As I kicked and punched it swung high with the force of the kicks and almost reaching the ceiling. Ginger watched impassively as he rested about five minutes between his sets. I was happy to put on a bit of a show. After about twenty minutes I felt hungry again and decided to finish up. Ginger got up, wandered across to the bag, drew his right fist back quite slowly and then CRACK. He had split his feet fore and aft in a blur and driven a punch deep into the bag. It didn't move; it *folded double* and split down the main seam so sawdust now trickled out. He just smiled, picked up his towel and walked out.

I mentioned what happened upstairs and was told the local legend about Ginger's daughter. Apparently she had been having trouble with a violent boyfriend. Ginger had cornered him one night and smashed his car roof into a V shape with his bare hands. Seeing that punch it was very easy to believe it. I'd met many strong people in karate, but I'd met few who could punch that hard. I was amazed at the sheer power he had displayed without any formal combat training. I was now fully committed to adding strength *and* power training to my weekly routine. I went to Sugars with Max regularly, and as Ginger recommended I perfect the Clean and Jerk to build my explosive power, I practised it night after night at work in the grimy downstairs gym with only the mortally wounded punchbag to inspire me.

I knew if I could get anywhere near as strong as Max or even half as explosive as Ginger, when added to my stamina and technical skills I would have all the right ingredients. My doorwork had also added a new ferocity to my fighting. In the dojo, if I caught people I obviously never finished them off, but apologised and backed off to let them recover. It had been hard until now to change that thinking in a Tournament. The ability to 'finish the job' had been essential on the door and I was now far more ruthless. I was confident I would not hold back again. The desire to prove people wrong also gave me a real focus. I had increasing self-belief. I just needed to bind all these attributes together to make myself a complete knockdown fighter.

Charnwood Dojo

Money was tight. My mortgage was biting hard, and my gym fees and food bills were running high. I had quit nightclubbing now after my doorwork experiences, but needed to earn more money so I could still travel down to train at squads and at other dojo around the country. I had moved near to Loughborough where a new Leisure Centre was due to open in September 1980. On speaking to some friends over dinner, one suggested teaching karate there and it seemed like a brilliant idea. I was only 24 but had been training for nine years and teaching for five. I had taught the lower grades at Leicester so I knew how to structure and run classes at that level and any revenue raised could support my own development. That sounded perfect!

On mentioning this to Pete he was pretty lukewarm about the whole idea. He mentioned 'branch-dojo' and such like, but I wanted to stand alone rather than continue feeding funds into the money-monster that Leicester dojo had become. The dojo was being extended to cover the two upstairs floors and include a TV lounge, sauna, showers, weight room, matted dojo, upstairs dojo and car park. This would all cost a fortune and I can understand his plight. He had made a fantastic place to train in, but now had the huge financial stress that went along with it. To me though, surroundings were by now irrelevant. I wanted the best coaching I could get, not the best facilities. I had to travel to learn from instructors who could take my skills further, which my new dojo would now help pay for.

I applied to the BKK and was accepted as a dojo operator, teaching twice a week in the new sports hall at Charnwood Leisure Centre. I little realised then that this would go on to provide so many years of enjoyment and good times.

Building Up

With six months to go I got started. I had a check list of targets that I struck off once achieved. The physical ones were easy. Timed runs through a local park for stamina. Bench pressing my bodyweight ten times - not hugely strong in real terms but a massive step-up from last year. Squatting one and a half times my bodyweight ten times. Cleaning and Jerking my bodyweight was far harder but I got there eventually. One by one the targets fell and with each one I felt more confident.

My training load was massive, far too much in hindsight but I knew nothing then about overtraining and such like. A typical week included training twice at Leicester on bag work and basics, teaching twice in Loughborough and four bodybuilding sessions with Max and Hubert, a young fighter from Leicester that Max was also helping. On top of that I ran around

Bradgate Park several mornings a week which although only just over four miles, included some really harsh climbs. On duty I sneaked off to the gym to practise my Olympic lifting, which my Watch Commander kindly turned a blind eye to. I also got my workmates to hold pads for me, which he didn't tolerate for long, after some got dead legs and a few bruises. I wonder now how I managed it, but all I seemed to do when I wasn't training or working was to eat and fall asleep. My social life was by now virtually non-existent. Everything else was put on hold so I could focus on my goal. It was years later before I realised I was structuring my weekly plan totally wrong, and half my sessions were in fact just cancelling each other out. *(Note: Work on speed or technique before working on strength, work on strength before working on endurance.)* For now though I pressed grimly on.

Sparring posed a few problems, as although Pete encouraged me and wanted me to do well, this stopped short of risking injuries to the Leicester members. By then I'd grown up a bit and was careful not to injure my sparring partners, but hard fighting clearly carries risks that 'dojo' sparring seeks to minimise. My solution was to recruit my members at Charnwood. Although we had only been going for about six months many could already hit really hard. I kept a few of the bigger and more capable ones back after normal training and did about twenty rounds of thirty seconds each with them back to back.

I asked them to go at me as hard as they possibly could. Some were big PE students from Loughborough University and good athletes in their own right so they really got stuck in. I would soak everything up for about 20 seconds, then explode back and score as quickly as I could. I took a lot of punishment, but the experience of riding out intense pressure without panicking and then scoring on my chosen targets was really useful. They all stuck to the task and kept giving me a hard time week after week and I honestly felt they loved doing it. Years later, Steve Hammond (a great friend and my longest suffering student) told me they all dreaded it for days beforehand. No-one got hurt - at least nothing more than bruising - and I respected them all the more for helping me out despite their fears.

I knew this still wouldn't give me the cutting edge I sought though, so I again asked Brian Fitkin if I could go back to Sweden to finish off my preparations. He was delighted to help. Despite being nervous recalling how hard the sparring had been in 1978, I knew I needed to test myself against the best fighters possible. His student, Hans Lundgren (now known as Dolph Lundgren of Hollywood fame) would also be there, along with Kurt Pettersson who I had been disqualified against the previous year. As I got on the plane my stomach was doing somersaults, *but I still got on.* Just winning that private battle told me I had now come a long, long way from the scared little lad who always ran and hid when his father got angry.

Mental Strength

People have asked me many times over the years, 'Why Sweden? Weren't there enough good fighters here?' Of course there were, but as I already knew many of them from squads and Tournaments I wanted to go that bit further. Howard Collins always prepared for Tournaments in New York, as the intensity and change of surroundings focused the mind in a way training locally could never quite do. Of course, everyone is different. Some may prefer home comfort and the support of their loved ones, but for me I wanted a more Spartan regime.

Mental strength, as in the ability to focus and keep trying, is a trainable asset. I found that for me, a planned sequence of successively more difficult training and sparring goals helped me the best, with sparring with Brian again at the very top of the list. In many ways this was not a new idea. My father had told me years before how his training duties meant building up Royal Marine recruits gradually until they exceeded in training what they would be expected to do in their commando tests. In the Fire Brigade we started on short extension ladders then moved on to gradually higher ones until eventually climbing 100 foot Turntable ladders without fear. That would have been impossible without a gradual and progressive build up. I applied the same methodology to the Tournament. Although I had already fought for years I wanted to build up again to the challenge I had faced in my first trip to Sweden. Sure, it would be tough, but pressure makes you grow while nerves and stress can only destroy you. Having once again trained and fought with Brian in Stockholm, I reasoned facing people nearer my own standard at home would be far easier on the mind.

The weight categories had now been changed. Instead of being 'Heavyweight' at anything over 80 kilograms, there would now be a 'Light heavyweight' category from 78 to 86. I had put on a few slabs of muscle where previously there had been skin and bone, not least on my abdominals as endless sit-ups had been dropped in favour of roman chair work holding a 50 lb weight. Having lost three times to body punches I wanted to plug that gap for sure. I was still comfortably less than 86 kilograms though despite eating for England every single day. I have no idea why the categories were changed, but as I had started my build up long before this was announced it did not affect my decision to enter either way. I was obviously happy enough about not having to face the awesome Hans Lundgren who stood out as exceptional, narrowly losing in Japan to Makoto Nakamura, the two-times World Champion.

In my category though I would face the likes of Jeff Whybrow, Vince Halliday, Roy Banton, Kurt Pettersson and a new and exciting fighter from northern Sweden, Michael Söderkvist who had trained and fought in Japan and was reputedly very talented. In truth anyone there was capable of winning. In a pool of 32, luck obviously plays a part. Hard fights in the early rounds might mean injuries or exhaustion later, so the only way to prepare was to cut no corners and get in the best shape possible. The top fighters in any discipline are superb athletes, and in knockdown the ability to take and ignore punishment through five rounds of hard fighting sorts the men from the boys.

On arrival in Sweden I went straight to the dojo to find the squad raring to go. We were to train every day in the mid-morning for about 90 minutes. This was intense, but after the sheer volume of work I had been doing, I felt strong and fresh every time. In the first session Brian put me on a bag for five minutes to warm up.

Anxious to impress, I hit it with every technique I could think of, from every conceivable angle. On stopping, he just said, 'You're doing too much.' I was confused, as having a broad range of skills seemed beneficial, but he then patiently explained that it's not about how many techniques you can do, but more about selecting the most effective *for you* and focusing on ways to apply them with a much higher rate of success.

We constructed an imaginary pyramid. Techniques that I could reliably deliver explosively on target were at the top. Next below these were those to be used if the opportunity arose, and finally came any others that would not feature in any pre-planned way, except if injuries caused a revision of my tactics. Training and partner work focused entirely on getting the best techniques grooved in as automatic and reflex actions. We drilled them over and over until they were explosive and reliable. Sparring obviously took into account that an injury at this late stage would be disastrous, and despite getting a few knocks and bumps, not least to my nose (again) I had no injury problems.

Stockholms Karate Kai had a huge and well equipped gym and as we were not required to attend normal classes, I maintained my strength levels in the evenings. One of the best parts for me was going running with Hans and Kurt. We ran a few miles at a brisk pace and then did repeated uphill sprints on a steep twisty path about 150 metres long. To my delight and to Brian's amazement I beat them every time, as being smaller and more agile now became a distinct advantage. At the last sparring session I caught Brian with a strong front kick. He grunted. I tried it again, caught him squarely and to my amazement he sank to the floor on one knee. I had winded him the first time I connected and the second one immediately afterwards had compounded the effect. I was stunned. Let me quickly say I doubt I'd have got near Brian had he been going his hardest instead of helping me prepare, but like the gentleman he is he took it in the right spirit and didn't feel the need to punish me afterwards. I thank him for that.

On the way back to England I pondered my progress. Ten years ago, when I started training I had been scared stiff of getting hurt. I then got fitter but in my first competitions I worried too much about letting others down. I then got more confident, but lacking real impact I often hoped to wear opponents down rather than knock them down and so get through on a judges decision. I had now added power and learnt to be ruthless and finish off opponents as soon as possible. I was now fitter, stronger and more mature. Perhaps most important, I had now selected and drilled my best techniques until they were formidable and reliable weapons.

I now felt totally relaxed and completely prepared in mind, body and spirit for the first time ever leading up to a major Tournament. I was ready for anyone. Bring it on!

British Champion

I stayed with friends near to London the night before to ease the journey down, and slept like a baby in a huge bed. We drove down easily and arrived in good time. In the first years I fought I had always rushed to the toilets on arrival hoping desperately that there was toilet paper available. I then wised up and took my own. Now I didn't need the toilet, another small indication of progress I suppose. Firemen love practical jokes, so I briefly considered *removing* the toilet rolls from the main changing rooms *for a laugh.* I decided against that as it seemed rather unsporting, but it again showed how relaxed I felt. I saw young fighters rushing into the toilets and smiled to myself remembering how I used to be just like that. I then thought *hang on a minute, I'm too relaxed here,* and started to focus and visualise my fights. In my mind they all ended with a knockout.

The British and International Open Knockdown Championships at Crystal Palace in London was for years the premier Kyokushin Tournament outside Japan. Fighters entered from all over Europe, Scandinavia, the Middle East, Africa and even several Americans travelled over to test their skills. Into this mix were then added many famous names from other karate styles, most of whom left badly bruised and shocked at the sheer ferocity of knockdown fighting. There were often over 100 fighters spread across the categories and in 1981 there would be 32 in the Light heavyweights. I had previously gone to look at the draw on arrival, but this year I didn't bother - which again showed a new confidence.

Years later I was to read about the Spartans. They were so confident of their tactics they never changed them. It didn't matter who they faced, they were so highly trained they stuck to their own battle-plans every time rather than making things up on the day. That is exactly how I felt. Instead of wondering and stressing about what my opponents *might* do, I focused calmly and entirely on what I *would* do to them. This stage of development is a milestone for a fighter, as it signals a predatory mindset. I no longer concerned myself in any way about how things would look or what I would consciously choose. All the tools I needed were sharp and I just had *let's get this done* as my goal. Chance, as they say, favours the prepared mind.

The Charnwood members arrived and set up in an area of the seating that for the rest of the day would be part of Loughborough. The noise they made was incredible, and certainly got my new dojo noticed. As they started chanting I heard one Sarf Landan boy ask, 'Where the faks Charn-wood?'

They certainly knew by the end of the day. The fighting started with the Lightweights on all three areas so I had a while to wait. This had been a tense time previously, but I now ate sparingly and relaxed with my Walkman, sipping water to keep hydrated. I had warmed up and stretched on arrival and was good to go. I noticed many fighters prowling around constantly banging pads. These outward shows of aggression and energy I knew and recognised as simply attempts to conceal and control their very corrosive nerves. Some glared at me, I smiled back. The Swedish team had arrived and I wished them all well, meeting Michael Söderkvist for the first time. Studying his body language later I saw that he too radiated a quiet steady confidence. I wondered impassively whether we would meet. Maybe it was a premonition.

At last the Light Heavyweights were told to

prepare, and my name was called up. I was to face a Wu-Shu fighter I had never seen before. The Wu-Shu group had entered for years and were by now a force to be reckoned with. They also brought a huge crowd with them. They had been asked already that day to keep things civil and show respect to their fighter's opponents and the match officials. As we faced each other I heard some remarks thrown my way and thought *I'm going to love this.* My opponent danced around a bit and tried a high left roundhouse kick. I blocked it easily and as his leg come down I switch stepped and hit his front leg with a huge inside thigh kick, lifting it high into the air. He brought it down but looked shocked and off-balance, so I followed up by hooking both hands either side of his neck and pulling his head straight down onto a solid knee kick. He shot back up and stood motionless for a second, before slowly turning away and crashing down at full stretch onto the mat. The Charnwood crowd went mad, but the Wu-Shu boys were completely silenced. It had taken about ten seconds from 'Hajime' to knockout.

(Note: 'Hooking' meant keeping the palms horizontal and applying pressure with the edges of the hands. 'Grabbing' was with the palms vertical and applying pressure with the fingers, and was illegal. I had practised this move correctly repeatedly after my disqualification in the 1980 team match.)

I followed my opponent to the sick bay and offered him my hand. He shook it sportingly and wished me good luck. His nose was broken and he seemed in a lot of pain, but was man enough to offer no complaint. I returned to the seating area glad to be finally off the mark. People I had never met before now started crowding around asking endless questions. I tried to respond politely but needed to remain focused. The boards were being set up for the breaking and I was due to line up. I had already decided not to risk injury in the breaking. My thinking was simple. I planned to win every fight convincingly, so I would never need to rely on having broken more boards. I lined up alongside my next opponent, who to my amazement had put up five boards. A tremendous break if he pulled it off, but as the saying goes, 'Boards don't hit back' so pretty meaningless in our coming fight. He made some flippant comment about how hard he would be punching my ribs. I felt my hackles rise and imagined the pleasure I'd get kneeing him in the face, but he then saved me the trouble by breaking his hand on the boards which obligingly held firm. He then tried the minimum of two and failed those as well. I broke two, went back to my seat, put my feet up and picked up a magazine. He went for an x-ray.

His failure put me straight through to the last eight, along with Vince Halliday, Roy Banton, Kurt Pettersson, Jeff Whybrow, Michael Söderkvist and two of Steve Arneil's students, one from Crawley whose name escapes me, and Glen Eldon, a new and very strong fighter from Wimbledon. As we lined up to break with *shuto,* we had the biggest shock of the day. Jeff Whybrow was Michael Söderkvist's next opponent and the crowd was eagerly anticipating their fight. Jeff was considered a breaking expert. He regularly did fantastic demonstrations and the crowd just groaned when he failed four boards. He then had to go back to the minimum of two, which he casually flicked at, only to recoil in horror when they didn't break. Maybe they were rogue boards, but in truth I think he just treated 'only two' with contempt and paid a huge price. I broke two again and resumed my seat.

As I walked back I had noticed my next opponent had a slight limp. On being called up he hobbled to the mat and the referee announced he had withdrawn due to injury. His coach later told me he didn't fancy the job as he was slightly injured, which goes to show the devastating effects that a fast knockout can have on your *future* opponents confidence. That simple ten second first fight had in fact scored two *Ippons.* (Full scores) One on the mat and one before my opponent even got up there. In the meantime Vince and Glen smashed each other up in a real battle with Glen emerging the victor but suffering terribly to do so. Roy and Kurt had another war; with Roy winning narrowly despite a penalty for punching Kurt so hard in the face he smashed his teeth and split his own knuckle to the bone. Since face punches in theory merited instant disqualification, how he got through was questionable indeed. Meanwhile Michael and I sat, waited and relaxed. Fate was drawing us ever closer. I would face Roy in the semi-final while Michael would face Glen. Roy came over to me moaning bitterly about my having 'byes' while he had had three hard fights. It was out of my hands. I had trained hard and was willing to fight anyone but fate, for once, was going my way. I had had hard draws in the past, not least against Howard Collins, but never moaned about it at the time, especially not to other fighters. In view of the fact he'd not been disqualified, I pointed out we'd both been very lucky already. I now really wanted to spoil his day.

We were now safely through to the evening finals. The two outer areas were cleared away leaving one central mat. After the demonstrations, the place was packed with four thousand eager spectators; VIPs and even a Jordanian Prince with his twitchy bodyguards. I started to notice the strangest sensations. Colours seemed unusually bright, coffee smelt great and a hasty sandwich tasted more delicious than ever before. I felt almost light-headed, totally relaxed yet laser focused. I could read a program someone was holding a few rows in front. This seemed surreal. Psychologists talk of the 'flow' state and being in the 'zone'. I didn't understand those terms then but I felt that every single cell in my body had somehow linked hands and was driving me forwards with unstoppable force. If they'd brought King Kong in at that point I'd have dropped him. I felt immortal.

As they called me up to fight Roy, I noticed how bright the lights were and how cool the mats felt on my feet. Roy looked tired but determined. He was a superb fighter but I pushed him all over the mat. To his credit he never buckled. I gave him tremendous punishment but he fought on gamely. I felt so in charge though that for devilment I repeatedly lined him up with his coach and drove him off the mat until they tangled together. At the flags I won 5:0. I congratulated Roy, who rather ungraciously later claimed I would never have beaten him had he not been tired from facing Kurt in the previous round. Who knows? I do know I was fit enough to face anybody without complaint, so maybe Roy's preparation had not been so rigorous and he needed an excuse to ease his own disappointment. He came back two years later to win in fine style. He had his day then, but for now I was determined this one was going to be mine. Michael Söderkvist had by now beaten Glen Eldon and I saluted him as he left the mat. He waved back in good humour and I looked forward to testing myself against probably the coolest and most stylish man there.

The final duly came and I felt with real clarity that this was my time. I had studied Michael's style throughout the day. He fought left foot forward with his right hand close to protect the jaw and his left out antenna style, gauging his distance for his extremely fast roundhouse kicks. We exchanged many fast blows, both blocking and avoiding them easily. For the first minute we were very evenly matched. He then came in close and my hand brushed his face. He turned away as his contact lens had been dislodged. As he re-set it the judges conferred and I felt nerves for the first time, as it would have been cruel indeed if I was disqualified for accidental face contact. The referee returned and announced no penalty. We shook hands sportingly and got back to it. I never heard a sound from the crowd, but was told later the Charnwood boys were lifting the roof with, 'Charn-wood! Charn-wood!' drowning out the referee until the announcer had to ask them to quieten down a little.

At that point Michael tried a high left roundhouse kick. I blocked it with my right hand and lifted the leg slightly with my wrist. He leaned back a fraction to keep his balance and I managed to sweep his standing foot towards me with my left foot as I pushed his kicking leg upwards. He dropped at my feet and I threw a controlled follow-up punch to the body and looked to the referee. After what seemed an age I noticed two judges' flags shoot out level to the floor and he indicated 'Wazari.' There was about thirty seconds to go, during which we stood toe to toe and threw everything at each other while Michael desperately tried to level the score, but on the bell, as the little red bag was thrown in to end the fight I was half a point up and the new British and International Open Light Heavyweight Knockdown Champion. I had done it!

For the first time ever Pete had been on my side of the mat. I was happy to have him there with our previous differences forgotten. Perhaps ironically in view of the massive help he'd given me, Sensei Fitkin - as Swedish National Coach - had been on Michael's. They shook hands warmly as old friends and Michael and I bowed deeply to each other. He was a superb sportsman and fighting him was a real pleasure with no malice or trickery on either side, just hard and respectful combat - as it should be. I was presented with a replica Samurai Helmet as a trophy, and on lifting it to acknowledge the crowd one of the first people I noticed applauding was Vince Halliday.

Now the party really started. One of my students had brought a small bottle of Champagne, which was hastily opened and passed to the edge of the mat. So not to offend protocol I asked Pete to hold it as I posed for photographs with Steve Arneil, who congratulated me for sticking with it over the years until I had won. By the time I returned, Pete had drunk the lot. He was welcome to it, as I needed no alcoholic high at all; I was already floating on air. I had proved his harsh comments wrong and at last shaken that monkey off my back. I later jogged up the seats to a payphone to ring my parents, despite the fact it was by now nearly midnight. My father answered the phone. 'Hey! It's Gary. I've just won the Tournament!' I shouted over the noise. 'What the hell are you ringing at this time of night for?' he asked. 'Is this urgent?' I had to laugh. 'No, nothing desperate, I'll call you tomorrow.' I didn't care anymore, and suddenly realised that for all this time I had been fighting to prove things to myself, not to others.

Over the next few years Vince lost to Michael but beat Roy and Jeff. Michael beat Vince but lost to Roy who I had already beaten. Roy beat Michael but lost to Vince. Jeff lost to Vince and stopped fighting but returned unexpectedly in 1989 and won the middleweight division in fine style. I mention this merely to show that in truth we were all fairly close in our abilities and we all had our day in the sun. I really enjoyed mine.

British Champion

Moral Fibre

Did winning make me totally confident and fearless? Of course not! Fear is a natural response and finding confidence and self-belief in one area of life does not necessarily mean instant fearlessness in all others. Everyone hopes they will have the courage to face danger, but most wait until danger stares them in the face before they find out if they can cope. In the Fire Service danger goes with the job, so 'lacking moral fibre' is not something you would ever want your crew mates to say or think about you. No-one would want to partner up and enter a burning building with someone who was shaking with fear or looking for a toilet. Combat sport *does* give you effective strategies to control your nerves and your body's response to fear. These can then be applied in other areas of life. I found in the Fire Service I was now calmer and more focused when entering dangerous incidents. I simply never got scared to the point that I couldn't function. If things got 'exciting' I could control my breathing and focus on the task, rather than allow my imagination to spiral away. Courage is the ability to control fear and keep going forwards, not some magical ability to eliminate it completely. The Leicestershire Fire Service motto was well chosen: - For'ard For'ard

What produces a champion? Proper coaching is obviously important, as is functional training with intensity over time. First and foremost though is the will to win. The refusal to give up until you achieve your goal. The decision to push through setbacks and do everything in your power to ensure victory. Once this mindset takes over, mere physical considerations like genetics and natural talent take second place - but only if you want it badly enough.

I had now climbed my mountain and didn't need to climb it again. Others may chase titles and trophies for their own sake and I wish them well, but for me, getting to the top had answered any lingering doubts or questions I had about myself. I was then happy to focus on other parts of my life and training that had been held in limbo while getting there. I had a club full of enthusiastic students, a demanding job and a busy social life to catch up on. I also needed a break. I had overtrained for years and had injuries that just weren't healing up, so a complete rest was required until I was back to good health.

Two years later I went back to watch the Tournament. I had just been involved in a dramatic rescue at work and been praised by the Chief Fire Officer for my actions at the scene. During the day I was approached by Lloyd Payne, a pugnacious character who had won the lightweight division in the same year I had won the light heavyweights. He was a professional instructor, so karate was his work while for me it was 'just' a challenging hobby that enhanced the rest of my life. He asked his question in a way that actually made it a blunt statement. 'Is this right? You've bottled out of knockdown!' I thought back to the recent rescue, where despite *real* fear and danger several lives had been saved, and calmly replied that I had already achieved my aims. He looked puzzled, as to him one trophy or title could never have been enough.

I felt no need to explain any further. I had found what I was looking for. It was there all along, I just needed a way to bring it through. Knockdown was the perfect way for me. Man to man, with respect, against tough and well-trained opponents. I will always be grateful for the lessons learned along the way.

Comments welcome on gjec@btinternet.com

39341775R00080

Made in the USA
Lexington, KY
19 February 2015